KNIGHTS OF THE AIR

TIME
LIFE ®
BOOKS

This volume is one of a series that traces the adventure and science of aviation, from the earliest manned balloon ascension through the era of jet flight.

KNIGHTS OF THE AIR

by Ezra Bowen

AND THE EDITORS OF TIME-LIFE BOOKS

TIME-LIFE BOOKS, ALEXANDRIA, VIRGINIA

THE AUTHOR

Ezra Bowen writes from a lifelong interest in
World War I. In three decades as a journalist,
author and historian he has been a senior
editor of *Sports Illustrated,* an assistant managing editor of Time-Life Books and editor-
in-chief of American Heritage Books. His
half-dozen previous volumes include three
for Time-Life Books: *Wheels, The Middle Atlantic States* and *The High Sierra.* He was
also editor of two Time-Life Books series,
This Fabulous Century and The Old West.

THE CONSULTANTS for Knights of the Air

Walter J. Boyne, a retired United States Air
Force colonel, is Assistant Director of the National Air and Space Museum in Washington.
He has been a student of aviation history for
more than 40 years and has written more
than 150 articles in this field.

John McIntosh Bruce, who received a master
of arts degree from the University of Edin-
burgh, is the author of many authoritative
books and articles on historic aircraft. A former Royal Air Force pilot, he is Keeper of
Aircraft and Research Studies at the RAF
Museum, Hendon, London. He also serves
as Chairman, Historical Group Committee,
Royal Aeronautical Society, and is Vice President of Cross and Cockade, Great Britain.

THE CONSULTANTS for The Epic of Flight

Melvin B. Zisfein, the principal consultant, is
Deputy Director of the National Air and
Space Museum, Washington. He received
degrees in aeronautical engineering from the
Massachusetts Institute of Technology and
has contributed to many scientific, techno-
logical and historical publications. He is an
Associate Fellow of the American Institute of
Aeronautics and Astronautics.

Charles Harvard Gibbs-Smith, Research Fellow at the Science Museum, London, and
a Keeper-Emeritus of the Victoria and Albert Museum, London, has written or edited
some 20 books on aeronautical history. In
1978 he served as the first Lindbergh Professor of Aerospace History at the National Air
and Space Museum, Washington.

Dr. Hidemasa Kimura, honorary professor at
Nippon University, Tokyo, is the author of
numerous books on the history of aviation
and is a widely known authority on aeronautical engineering and aircraft design. One
plane that he designed established a world
distance record in 1938.

For information about any Time-Life book, please write:
Reader Information
Time-Life Books
541 North Fairbanks Court
Chicago, Illinois 60611

Library of Congress Cataloguing in Publication Data
Bowen, Ezra.
    Knights of the air.
    (Epic of flight; 1)
    Bibliography: p.
    Includes index.
    1. European War, 1914-1918—Aerial operations.
I. Time-Life Books. II. Title. III. Series.
D600.B64   940.4'4   79-9398
ISBN 0-8094-3252-8
ISBN 0-8094-3251-X lib. bdg.
ISBN 0-8094-3250-1 retail ed.

CONTENTS

Saber-bearing French cavalrymen are overtaken by a solitary biplane on its way to the front in World War I. The airplane was making

Cavalry's leap to the skies

"War in the air," trumpeted a poster for Britain's Royal Flying Corps, "recalls the olden times, when knights rode forth to battle and won honor and glory by their deeds of personal heroism." The fledgling military air services of World War I had no trouble finding volunteers for a life that promised "romance, action, adventure, and opportunities for glorious achievement." Many recruits were cavalrymen who had seen their traditional role as the swashbucklers of war usurped almost overnight by the airmen in their outlandish but far-ranging new flying machines.

The glamorized promise of the poster did not entirely misrepresent the lot of the World War I aviator. He flew into battle high above the barbed wire and boredom, the mud and mass death of the ground war below. On occasion his plane, like the arms of the medieval knights, carried the blessing of the clergy; his chances for "deeds of heroism" were many and his feats were glorified proportionately far beyond those of his comrades in the trenches. But, like them, he died—his job ironically made more deadly by that same search for glory.

Honors accrued to a pilot in proportion to how many of his kind in enemy uniform he shot down. What began as a chivalrous adventure became an increasingly lethal and unglamorous enterprise, with little mercy shown for an overmatched or disabled foe. Before the Great War ended, one much-decorated knight of the air declared that, if anything, he felt like a "hired assassin."

its first appearance in a major war, the cavalry one of its last.

In a ceremony harking back a thousand years, when a knight's lance and sword were blessed before he went into battle, a Catholic

priest sprinkles holy water on a Blériot monoplane at an Allied airfield with the French pilot and his fellow aviators in attendance.

A squadron of British Bristols flies into the evening sky over the Western Front. Formation flying, which began as a defensive measure to

protect reconnaissance planes, was soon adopted by pursuit planes, which often attacked as a team, then broke off into individual duels.

The dogfight became World War I's equivalent to the medieval duel, with results far more likely to be fatal. In this rare example of

air-to-air combat photography, a victorious German fighter watches as an Allied two-seater goes down trailing a plume of smoke.

A fallen British aviator is carried from his wrecked plane by Allied soldiers. Many proud fliers scorned parachutes as affronts to their

valor, and the Allied high command discouraged their use in any case, on the principle that "a pilot's job is to stick to his aeroplane."

1

The rush to join a "noble cause"

On the beach at Biarritz, 19-year-old Georges Guynemer was idling away the soft summer days of 1914 gazing at the sky, his eyes occasionally seeking the approach of one of the exotic new flying machines that favored the strand as a landing place. On August 2, a Sunday, he was jolted from his reverie by the news that war had broken out. Guynemer, the son of a former army officer, rushed to enlist. Twice the recruiting officer turned him down: He was too frail for the infantry or the cavalry. Passionately anxious to serve, he sought a third route into uniform—as a student mechanic in his country's newest military arm, the flying service.

In Owen Sound, Ontario, William "Billy" Bishop, just turned 20, was awaiting his impending dismissal from Canada's Royal Military College. Staff officers considered Bishop the worst cadet the academy had ever had—a rebellious brawler and a hopeless scholar. Now, however, Canada too was going to war, and the emergency generated instant forgiveness. Bishop soon found himself in England, with a commission as lieutenant of cavalry. There for the first time he saw a British military airplane take off from a field. That, he decided, was "the only way to fight a war; up there above the mud and the mist in the everlasting sunshine."

At Strasbourg, Germany, Ernst Udet sat down to write a letter to his father, the dominant figure in his 18-year-old life. Ernst wanted to be an artist, but the elder Udet had goaded him into "manlier" pursuits; he had joined the Aero Club of Munich and flew the club's first glider, which he promptly cracked up. Now the War was three weeks old and Ernst, along with a generation of young Germans, had been ordered into battle. "You have often accused me of cowardice," he wrote, "but I think you were wrong. I am off tomorrow to the front. If I happen to be killed, then my frivolous life will have met a worthy end."

Across half the world during this fateful summer, thousands of such young men were swept up by the currents of war. Edward "Mick" Mannock, a British citizen working in Constantinople on a telephone project, was tossed into a Turkish jail as an enemy alien and so maltreated that, when repatriated to England five months later, he was found unfit for military duty. But his hatred for the enemy so obsessed him that he haunted recruiting offices until someone accepted him.

In England, a husky young American, Victor Chapman, Harvard class of '13, heard Londoners singing the French "Marseillaise" in the

Captivated by the alluring call to fly and fight, England's Richard Raymond-Barker, just turned 21, was one of thousands of young men to volunteer for air service in the first year of World War I. In 1918 he was the last man killed by the War's leading ace, Germany's Manfred von Richthofen.

streets. Informing his millionaire father of his determination to fight "for the most noble of all causes," he enlisted in the French Foreign Legion and within the week was digging trenches for the defense of Paris.

Eastward across Europe, cavalry Lieutenant Manfred von Richthofen was overdue from a patrol into Russian-occupied Poland. His colleagues in an elite uhlan regiment reported his death to his father, a Prussian baron. But the report was premature. Richthofen was hiding in a churchyard, waiting for a force of Cossack horsemen to go away. Soon he rode safely back across the border.

Mannock, Chapman, Richthofen and all the others were destined for immortality for their part in a wholly new kind of warfare: aerial combat. Europe was plunging into a military disaster worse than any it had ever known. In a span of four years, 30 million men would be killed or wounded. Most of the dead would be lost forever in the anonymity of mass and mud. But the military airmen were seen—and saw themselves—as a breed apart. Men also died in the sky, but up there a man's daring, or lack of it, was visible to all, and the issues were clearly resolved. The battle ended when the loser crashed to earth while the victor was still flying high.

From the beginning, the intrepid young airmen inspired legends. Some of the tales were exaggerated yarns created for propaganda or profit. But enough of the fliers' unprecedented experiences were verifiable to make exaggeration unnecessary. They could recount dramatic stories of individual heroism, of brushes with death and miraculous escapes, of raucous off-duty escapades and of occasional gallantry reminiscent of an age long past.

They became a new kind of cavalry, conducting from up among the clouds the same sort of missions less-favored riders still executed amid the trees and the rocks. The fliers would swoop over the corpse-strewn trenches of Europe to strafe and bomb, to spy out enemy troop movements, to locate targets for the artillery and, most theatrically, to duel with the aerial cavalry of the other side.

Dashing and colorful—and young (their average age was about 20)—they were feared, feted and exalted as the reincarnations of medieval knights, professional killers with the manners of gentlemen and the courage of eagles. "They recall the legendary days of chivalry," declared Prime Minister Lloyd George of Britain, "not merely by the daring of their exploits but by the nobility of their spirit." Hundreds of the most stalwart fliers actually were knighted by their grateful nations. Manfred von Richthofen, for example, who abandoned his cavalry career to volunteer for the Air Service, was but one of fourscore German fliers designated a knight of the order Pour le Mérite by Kaiser Wilhelm II for repeated heroism in the air.

Although the appellation of knight was widely applied to them, the great pilots more commonly came to be known as aces. The term at first meant an excellent flier, a high card to play against the enemy. But

Three years before World War I began, the airplane made its military debut in North Africa during a colonial altercation between Italy and Turkey. A contemporary postcard (above) shows the "Spirit of Italy" guiding warships and three fanciful aircraft across the Mediterranean. Below, Arabs are confounded by their first look at the planes. One Italian pilot dropped four bombs "a little larger than oranges," causing few casualties but great consternation.

soon it denoted a pilot who had achieved a specific number of confirmed victories in the air.

The homage paid to the air aces was such as had not been meted out to simple fighting men for centuries. German ace Max Immelmann was invited to dinner with the King of Bavaria, and, he wrote, "the King of Saxony, the Crown Princes of Prussia and Saxony, the Chief of War Aviation, sent me telegrams of congratulations." French aces sometimes received gold watches and cash bounties for their kills: Guynemer collected 15,000 francs from the Michelin tire company (in a characteristically knightly gesture he turned the money over to a fund for the wounded). German supply sergeants traded precious fresh ham and sausage for autographed pictures of Richthofen. The superb German flight leader Oswald Boelcke was dogged for days on one triumphal tour by a 12-year-old boy who, Boelcke reported with astonishment, "knew the dates of all my victories."

Despite many shared characteristics, the pilots of World War I were a varied lot. Mick Mannock became a brooding hater who liked to close in tight on a kill so he could send the "German vermin to hell in flames." His countryman Albert Ball, on the other hand, said he felt "rotten" when his gunnery did its work. "I am really beginning to feel like a murderer," he wrote. "Shall be so pleased when I have finished." Ball was 20 when he recorded that thought. He did not see 21.

Georges Guynemer, who had undergone surgery for appendicitis at the beginning of the War, was chronically frail; once, he almost fainted at a troop review in his honor. By contrast, another French hero, Charles Nungesser, was an athlete of enormous vitality. A superb soccer player, boxer, swimmer and cyclist, he had trouble squeezing his muscular frame into the cockpit, and he kept flying with unflagging gusto despite an appalling series of wounds and injuries.

American ace Eddie Rickenbacker, who went into the War with his country in 1917, was a champion automobile racer who seemed to know how to fly the moment he put his hands on the controls. His equally celebrated flight leader, Raoul Lufbery, was at first so clumsy that his instructors almost rejected him.

Ernst Udet admitted to being so frightened in his early flights that he could not even fire his guns. But Billy Bishop flew with such joyful disregard that an awed comrade described him as "incapable of fear."

Manfred von Richthofen was a deadly tactician with a contempt for showy aerobatics. He preferred to fly in tight formation and kill with one straight pass from high up out of the sun. His brother Lothar was an incurable aerobat, ready to fire at anything in the sky.

By and large they were modest men—but France's René Fonck, who topped all Allied pilots with 75 confirmed victories, had a streak of braggadocio that did not always endear him to his comrades.

To lusty adventurers such as Nungesser and his sidekick Jean Navarre, the War often seemed a marvelous lark, the off-duty hours filled with fast cars, fascinating women and all the champagne a fellow could

Tentative approaches to air power

Gradually, as war approached, the future combatant nations of Europe began to take the flying machine seriously, and what had been primarily a civilian sport took on a military tinge.

In France, where aviation had generated enormous popular enthusiasm, the War Ministry ordered a Wright "Flyer" in 1909 and solicited domestically designed planes for military use. By late 1910, France had 30 aircraft in service and 52 military pilots, certified by the Aero Club of France, who performed creditably at that year's maneuvers. In 1912, the government launched a national fund-raising campaign that raised 4 million francs to finance the purchase of additional planes.

German aircraft development, overshadowed by the success of Count von Zeppelin's airships, proceeded slowly. At first German airplane manufacturers copied foreign designs, with and without license. Not surprisingly, the first German flying competitions, held to promote the domestic aircraft industry, were dominated by foreign entries, particularly those from France. Not until the Germans started their own national fund-raising campaign for aviation in 1912 did they begin to reduce the French lead.

Britain, even further behind, formed an Army Air Battalion in 1911 with a total of five aircraft and fewer than a dozen competent pilots. But the establishment of the Royal Flying Corps a year later was accompanied by a Parliamentary appropriation large enough to get British military aviation off the ground.

Austria-Hungary had the smallest military budget among the major powers and was least prepared for an air war. A Taube monoplane designed in Austria had become an international success by 1910, but only one Austrian firm was capable of producing it in quantity. On the eve of war, Austria-Hungary turned to Germany to stock its air force.

A Prussian cavalryman watches a German-built Wright biplane over Berlin-Johannisthal airfield during a national flying contest in 1910.

In 1911 the first graduating class of Austria-Hungary's Royal and Imperial flying school at Wiener Neustadt stands before a Taube monoplane designed by Austrian Igo Etrich. The plane was one of Austria-Hungary's fleet of five military aircraft.

French infantrymen and mechanics stand by a line of Maurice Farman biplanes during maneuvers in 1912. The planes made up Escadrille M.F.5, one of five squadrons then in service, each designated by the initials of the type of plane it flew.

A largely civilian crowd examines a Bristol Boxkite at the British Army's 1910 maneuvers as Captain Bertram Dickson prepares to take off.

drink. To others, war was lonely and joyless, and a number of aces never smoked, drank or caroused. The leading women in the lives of Immelmann and Richthofen seemed to be their mothers, to whom they wrote incessantly; Guynemer's closest confidante was his sister.

Each a distinct individual in a war that otherwise tended to smother individuality, the air fighters developed colorful and defiant escutcheons to carry into battle. The planes of the fearsome Canadian Black Flight took to the sky trimmed in that piratical hue, with names such as "Black Sheep," "Black Maria" and "Black Roger" painted on them. France's elite Stork Squadrons flew with the emblem of that bird emblazoned just behind their cockpits, as if daring anyone to shoot at it. After Udet had recovered from his neophyte's nerves, he became cocksure enough to inscribe the taunting words *Du doch nicht!!* (Certainly not you!!) on the elevator surfaces of his tail assembly. The most brazen—and respected—imagery of all was the throbbing red color of Richthofen's entire plane, probably the most celebrated single weapon of the War.

As practitioners of a new art, the pilots developed a new vocabulary. To Allied fliers, antiaircraft fire was "Archie," so named by a British pilot who encouraged himself whenever a shellburst rocked his plane by shouting "Archibald, certainly not!"—a London music-hall refrain sung as the show's leading lady fended off a lecherous suitor. The elongated gasbags that both sides used as observation balloons were called, inevitably, "sausages"; the fiery projectiles that ground batteries fired to protect the sausages were "flaming onions." A plane's single hand-operated control lever was dubbed a "joy stick." And of course a shoot-out between hostile aircraft became a "dogfight."

In a constant and usually losing effort to stay warm in open cockpits at altitudes that eventually reached 20,000 feet and more, the airmen adopted wonderfully distinctive clothing: goggled leather helmets, gloves of wolfhide, shaggy bearskin coats and even shaggier sheepskin boots, parkas, school sweaters and cavalry boots.

The fliers were inveterate pet collectors. Dogs and cats abounded at frontline airfields. René Fonck kept a stork named Helen, and a squadron of American volunteers who would become renowned as the Lafayette Escadrille adopted a pair of lion cubs. The only black American pilot of the War, Eugene Bullard, flew with a pet monkey tucked in his flying suit.

Even chivalry was an individual matter. Not long after he became an ace, Ernst Udet found himself dueling a French pilot whom he recognized to be the already-celebrated Guynemer. After some minutes of twisting and turning during which neither man could get in a clear shot, Udet's gun jammed. Seeing his foe hammering away at the breech, Guynemer waved and let him go home. But Edwin Parsons of the Lafayette Escadrille recalled that in most cases, "if the other fellow's guns jammed, you popped him off if you could."

The death of a pilot, particularly an ace, was attended by consider-

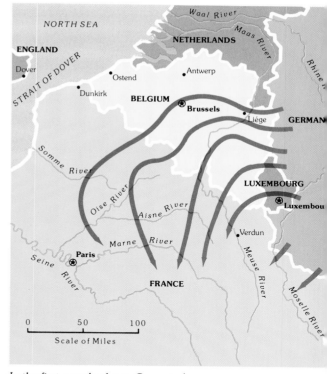

In the first month of war, Germany's armies (arrows) swept through Belgium, Luxembourg and northern France to within sight of Paris. Aided by air reconnaissance, the Allies turned back the German advance at the River Marne and both sides dug in.

able ritual. In British squadrons early in the War, a missing man's messmates would leave his chair empty for a period—and woe to the unwary replacement who sat in it before being granted permission. After the death of a renowned flier, enemy planes might fly over his field, dropping flowers and notes of regret. Told that he had killed the admired Werner Voss, British Lieutenant A. P. F. Rhys Davids blurted, "Oh if I could only have brought him down alive."

By the final year of the War such sentiment had all but vanished. The knights, after all, were instruments of carnage and they set some staggering records. Richthofen's 80 official kills led those of all other pilots in the War. Billy Bishop, propelled by a final sense of urgency, shot down 25 German aircraft during his last 12 days at the front. Fonck twice killed six in a single day and on one occasion shot down three in an incredible 10-second burst. Even more amazing was Canadian Major William George Barker's single-handed encounter, only two weeks before the War's end, with an estimated 50 to 60 German aircraft. With an epic

Four members of Belgium's air force, 37 pilots strong when the War began, rest beside their French-designed Farman H.F.20 biplane in October 1914. Though pushed to the sea by Germany's opening onslaught, the Belgians fought on. Fernand Jacquet, second from left, scored his nation's first air victory in April 1915.

boldness that earned him the Victoria Cross, Barker dispatched four of the German planes. Thrice wounded and semiconscious, he managed to dive clear of the remaining Germans and reach his own lines where he crash-landed, alive.

Many other young fliers never made it home. The statistics were appalling. The average life expectancy for a new airman on the Western Front was about three to six weeks. The French suffered a combat pilot loss of 77 per cent over the course of the War. Of the 180 Americans who volunteered to fly for France before the United States entered the War, almost half died or were captured. And the first squadrons of British pilots to go to France were informed that only one man in 20 could expect to see England again.

The feats of the airmen were the more remarkable because of the marvelous contraptions that carried them aloft. The airplane was even younger than the men who flew it. The War began scarcely more than a decade after the Wright brothers had launched their first "Flyer" across the sandy dunes at Kitty Hawk, North Carolina, in 1903. In those 10 or 11 years, aviation had made astonishing progress: The planes being flown at the outset of the Great War were rudimentary, but they embodied most of the basic elements an airplane would ever need: engine for power, wings for lift, propeller for thrust, tail for stability, fuselage to contain pilot and payload, and simple mechanisms to manually operate the movable parts—rudder, ailerons and elevators—needed for controlled flight.

Yet it was still a primitive machine with some unsettling characteristics. Most of the main structural members were thin pieces of hardwood, braced with steel wires. The pilot sat on a seat often made of wicker and placed directly atop the fuel tank. The skin was made of fabric stretched taut by a coat of highly flammable liquid called dope.

Though sturdier than they looked, some of these lightweight craft rattled and shook through the air as though they might come apart at any moment—and a number of them did. In the first months of war, Germany lost about 100 planes; most of the losses were due not to enemy action but to malfunctions and simple accidents.

Most World War I aircraft had no brakes. On the ground, a plane with its engine running had to be held back by crewmen until the pilot had revved up the engine for takeoff. At a signal, all hands then let go.

The average speed of a 1914 military airplane was about 60 miles per hour, at altitudes ranging from about 3,300 feet up to a giddy 12,000; flight duration varied from two to perhaps four hours, with about a third of that time taken up by laborious climbing and long, gliding descents. Few planes had controlled power; on landing, a pilot trying to slow his approach would keep turning his engine off and on by pressing a blip switch on the steering lever.

Many of the engines were water-cooled in-line designs scarcely different from automobile engines. But most were lightweight rotary de-

Compact and air-cooled by its own whirling motion, a rotary engine weighed less and vibrated less than early water-cooled engines. The nine cylinders of this 110 hp Oberursel rotary are aligned like spokes around a central crankcase. Visible inside the crankcase is a large off-center disc called the crankpin. Onto it bore the connecting rods of the pistons, which were driven by combustion in the cylinders and in turn caused the cylinders to rotate at high speed around a fixed crankshaft.

signs; unlike standard engines, in which the cylinders are fixed and the crankshaft rotates, the cylinders of a rotary engine whirled around a stationary shaft spewing a mist of odorous castor-oil lubricant.

The aviators' cynical, if cavalier, view of their machines was reflected in the last verse of a song popular in the Royal Flying Corps mess:

> Take the cylinder out of my kidneys,
> The connecting rod out of my brain, my brain,
> From the small of my back take the camshaft
> And assemble the engine again.

The grisly backdrop against which the knights of the air and their machines performed was not only the most devastating but, in many ways, the most poorly anticipated and most dimly understood war in the long chronicle of human conflict. It was a war that very few leaders appeared to want but for which most of Europe seemed in 1914 to be preparing—even, to a modest degree, in the air. During the final years of the build-up, the major powers had entered into alliances with one another and with lesser nations; they used these entanglements to play a perilous game of international cat's cradle with border lines and other prizes. Then, in 1914, the game came unstrung. On June 28, Archduke Franz Ferdinand, heir to the Austro-Hungarian empire, insisted, against all advice, on making a grand appearance in the recently annexed Bosnian city of Sarajevo. There he and his wife were shot by a 19-year-old Serbian terrorist named Gavrilo Princip.

A disastrous series of miscalculations followed. Austria blustered into war with Serbia; Russia, which had no real intention of launching a major fight, found itself committed on the side of Serbia—whereupon Germany, allied with Austria, declared war against both Russia and its recently acquired ally, France.

The week the War began, Germany sent two armies across neutral Belgium in a sweeping assault aimed down the coastal plain of France; its purpose was to outflank Paris and the French forces concentrated on the fortified common border with Germany. The strategy was excellent, based on a plan conceived years earlier by Count Alfred von Schlieffen. It strove to avoid a two-front land war by knocking out France before the anticipated Russian steam roller—really no more than a bottomless supply of manpower—could begin to move. But the slash through Belgium brought in the British Empire. It also lost for Germany much of whatever sympathy it enjoyed in the United States, whose population had swelled over the past decades with millions of immigrants; they had come from nations on both sides of the conflict, and most of them were determined to remain neutral.

By August 4, the line-up for the first war of global sweep was virtually complete: The alliance of France, Russia and Britain confronted the so-called Central Powers of Germany, Austria-Hungary and soon Turkey. Within a few weeks Japan and the following year Italy would join the Allies. Each of the land powers of Europe believed it could win quickly through bold infantry and cavalry attacks that would keep the enemy off balance. Britain, secure behind the world's finest navy, dispatched the bulk of its Army to the Continent in the firm belief, shared by every other belligerent, that the boys would be home by Christmas.

Those who did come home made it four blood-drenched years later. World War I would be the first to be fought on a massive scale with the instruments of the Industrial Revolution. In such a war the most courageous attack could not succeed against an army dug in behind barbed wire and equipped with the efficient, mass-produced weapons that came to dominate the mighty conflict: machine guns, fast-firing artillery, tanks and poison gas.

Like the soldiers on the ground, nearly all the early airmen went into combat with their minds still locked on ancient concepts of battle. Very few of the pilots or their commanders understood at first how their imperfect but potentially lethal machines should be used, or what their ultimate effect on warfare would be. A handful of prophets, however, already had made the case for air power.

An Italian staff officer named Giulio Douhet defined the fundamentals of air strategy in 1909. "The sky is about to become another battlefield no less important than the battlefields on land and sea," he wrote. "In order to conquer the air, it is necessary to deprive the enemy of all means of flying, by striking at him in the air, at his bases of operation, or at his production centers. We had better get accustomed to this idea," Douhet warned, "and prepare ourselves."

In 1911 Captain Bertram Dickson, the first British military officer to fly, foretold how airplanes would first be used, and how that use would expand: "Both sides would be equipped with large corps of aeroplanes, each trying to obtain information of the other"—in other words, they would be flying reconnaissance missions. "The efforts which each would exert in order to hinder or prevent the enemy from obtaining information" would lead to a war for the supremacy of the air "by armed aeroplanes against each other." Thus did Dickson predict the emergence of the fighter plane.

Another visionary, the French Captain Ferdinand Ferber, even explained how a dogfight would take place, with the hunter first climbing high like a hawk to pounce from above; how the intended victim would then "try, by means of a clever sideslip," to dodge, and finally, how he would come to ground, vanquished.

Count Helmuth von Moltke, Chief of the German General Staff, who would direct the wheeling flank movement across Belgium, also foresaw the military significance of aircraft. With characteristic precision, Moltke stated that by 1914 Germany should have an air force of 324 planes under independent command with "simple central authority such as is required by the needs and developments of the new arm."

But each of these prophets was snubbed, or worse, by his countrymen. Moltke was told by the German War Ministry that the Air Service and its machines were outside his jurisdiction. Ferber so irritated the

Italy's fascination with flight as an adventure of classic proportion is reflected in these wartime postcards from the school of military aviation at Cascina Malpensa.

French authorities that he was able to fly only when he was on leave, and then under an assumed name. Dickson found himself quietly ignored by British traditionalists. Colonel Douhet was castigated as a troublemaker and eventually cooled his heels for almost a year in an Italian jail cell.

The prophets of air power had little practical evidence to support their case. Single aircraft had occasionally been used as primitive bombers in local wars before 1914, but they had raised more dust than havoc, leading one less than prophetic American commentator to conclude that an aerial bomb was far less hazardous than "a falling aeroplane, or even a falling aviator."

When the War began, most people on earth—including an American officer named Mason Patrick, who would eventually lead the United States Air Service in Europe—had never seen a plane in flight. Nevertheless, considerable progress had actually been attained toward forging the airplane into an instrument of war. As early as 1907, the United States had set up the world's first military air arm, the Aeronautical Division of the Army Signal Corps; it was equipped in 1909 with a single Wright brothers plane. Americans also demonstrated the first parachute jump from a plane, created the first crude bombsight and in 1910 dropped the first aerial bomb—an artillery shell with fins—at an air meet above Tanforan race track in San Francisco. An airborne machine gun had been fired from a United States Army plane over College Park, Maryland, in 1912, scoring five hits on a six-by-seven-foot cheesecloth target but so alarming an official observer that he led a panicky dash of spectators to cover. "The continuance of such schemes can serve no practical purpose whatever," declared an Army spokesman, and further experiments in aerial gunnery were halted.

In Europe, attitudes changed faster—accelerated perhaps by the rising threat of war. In 1908, the Wright brothers had dazzled the Continent with demonstrations of their latest Flyer. The French, whose intrepid pioneer Louis Blériot flew across the English Channel in 1909, set about creating a fledgling aircraft industry. By 1913 a company founded by Raymond Saulnier and the brothers Robert and Léon Morane even experimented with a synchronizing device that would permit a machine gun to fire safely between whirling propeller blades.

Such activity alarmed the Germans. "Are we blind to what is going on before our eyes?" asked one periodical two years before the War began. Germany forthwith raised almost two million dollars for a campaign to train pilots and establish prizes for record-breaking flights. Some of the money went to a bright 22-year-old Dutchman named Anthony Fokker, who had come to Germany to finish his schooling and had stayed to open a flight school and to begin building airplanes on a shoestring. Some of the two million dollars was directed to an aircraft factory in Berlin where Franz Schneider, a Swiss-born engineer, was designing his own synchronized machine gun.

But Germany had its doubters too, including some who concluded that if indeed "the duty of the aviator is to see and not to fight," an airman could see a great deal better from the stable cabin of one of Count Ferdinand von Zeppelin's stately engine-powered dirigibles. For a dozen years these rigid-framed monsters had been floating imperturbably across the German sky. In 1909 they were organized into what amounted to the world's first commercial airline and by 1914 they had carried some 10,000 passengers at 40 miles per hour and better on 1,588 flights without a single fatality.

Britain's air power languished behind that of the Germans and French. Although a Royal Flying Corps had been organized in 1912 with a Central Flying School and a Royal Aircraft Factory, these units operated on so mean a budget that most of the early British aircraft, and some of their flight instructors as well, were a dubious collection of imports from France.

A training plane often had no cockpit, only a seat for the instructor and a perilous perch behind his back for the pupil. One future British air hero, Louis Strange, described his training thus:

"We knew nothing of the dual-control method of instruction. The pupil sat behind his instructor and could reach over his shoulder to grasp and use the control stick. There was, however, no way for the pupil to get his legs into contact with the rudder bar."

After a few such flights, instructor and pupil changed places, and in a very short time the neophyte tried his first solo. Strange got his pilot's license in three weeks.

When war burst over Europe, the British possessed 48 serviceable planes that could be sent across the Channel to the front. They were a motley mix of British-built craft and French Blériots and Farmans—the graceless bodies and wired landing skids of the latter having earned them the nickname "mechanical cows." On the eve of war, Britain's air force had been divided into two commands, the Royal Flying Corps and the Royal Naval Air Service; the latter, in staunch Navy tradition, exhibited a crusty pride about taking orders from anyone besides the Admiralty.

France was not much stronger. The French air service could scrape together five serviceable dirigibles and 138 aircraft. The planes were a grab bag of 11 models named for the firms that had produced them: two-seated Voisins, Farmans, Breguets and other biplanes with the engines in the rear acting as pushers, plus a number of front-engined Blériot and Morane-Saulnier "Parasol" monoplanes, the latter's wing set above the fuselage on an umbrella-like bracing of struts and wires.

At first French pilots were nearly all enlisted men with hardly more status than staff chauffeurs. Aloft they took orders from the observers, and since the planes possessed very noisy engines and no intercom systems, the process involved much futile shouting, frantic pointing and the passing of notes, many of which blew away in the wind.

Even Germany, with its formidable reputation for military efficiency

Learning from the ground up

If volunteers for air service were plentiful when war broke out, training facilities were not. Building on the few existing flying schools, the belligerents created dozens of new ones, refined training methods and found experienced pilots—including some brought home from battle—to teach the recruits. Students learned everything from plane construction to difficult tricks of flying, including looping, rolling, spinning and the climbing turn called a chandelle. And they were introduced to deflection shooting—how to hit a moving target from a moving craft (*overleaf*).

Not all survived the course. Over four years, Germany alone lost 1,800 airmen in training accidents. But if a pupil considered training hazardous, a British instructor warned, "let him find some other employment. Whatever risks he is asked to run here, he will have to run 100 times as many when he gets to France."

Aspiring British aviators study training manuals and working airplanes at a school in Oxford. A graduating pilot might have as many as 50 or as few as 12 hours in the air and was supposed to know how to dismantle and rebuild his plane.

Training in a prewar biplane, a British flying student in 1916 reaches from a perch behind the instructor to get the feel of the control lever.

A target plane is caught in the sight of a camera gun, a training device that shot film instead of bullets.

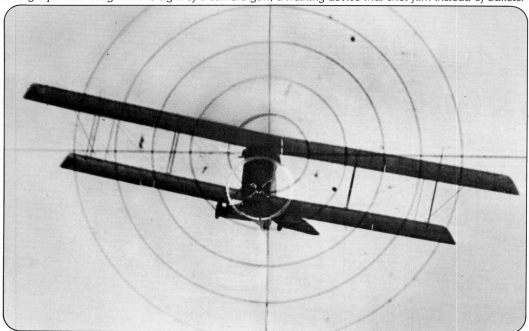

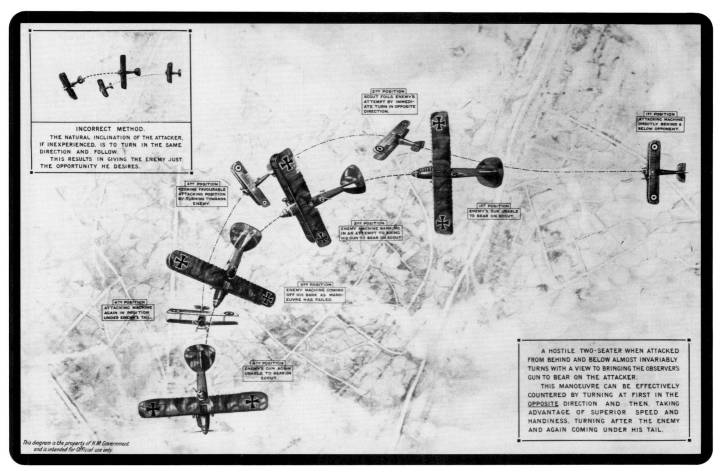

2ND POSITION
SCOUT FOILS ENEMY'S ATTEMPT BY IMMEDIATE TURN IN OPPOSITE DIRECTION.

1ST POSITION
ATTACKING MACHINE DIRECTLY BEHIND & BELOW OPPONENT.

3RD POSITION
REGAINS FAVOURABLE ATTACKING POSITION BY TURNING TOWARDS ENEMY.

1ST POSITION
ENEMY'S GUN UNABLE TO BEAR ON SCOUT.

2ND POSITION
ENEMY MACHINE BANKING IN AN ATTEMPT TO BRING HIS GUN TO BEAR ON SCOUT.

3RD POSITION
ENEMY MACHINE COMING OFF HIS BANK AS MANOEUVRE HAS FAILED.

4TH POSITION
ATTACKING MACHINE AGAIN IN POSITION UNDER ENEMY'S TAIL.

4TH POSITION
ENEMY'S GUN AGAIN UNABLE TO BEAR ON SCOUT.

A HOSTILE TWO-SEATER WHEN ATTACKED FROM BEHIND AND BELOW ALMOST INVARIABLY TURNS WITH A VIEW TO BRINGING THE OBSERVER'S GUN TO BEAR ON THE ATTACKER.
THIS MANOEUVRE CAN BE EFFECTIVELY COUNTERED BY TURNING AT FIRST IN THE OPPOSITE DIRECTION AND THEN, TAKING ADVANTAGE OF SUPERIOR SPEED AND HANDINESS, TURNING AFTER THE ENEMY AND AGAIN COMING UNDER HIS TAIL.

This diagram is the property of H.M.Government and is intended for Official use only.

A detailed British training poster illustrates the right and wrong ways to attack a German fighter plane from the rear and from below.

Learning how to shoot from a moving vehicle, a British airman fires his machine gun from a simulated cockpit that moves along rails.

on the ground, seemed mostly thumbs in the air. The observer was usually a cavalry officer with experience in traditional scouting but little or no training to alert him to the dramatic difference in the look of, say, a picket line of machine guns as seen from the ground and as viewed from 2,500 feet in the air. As a further handicap, many of Germany's 295 planes had such broad wings that the observer could barely see the ground. The German Air Service—including the four Zeppelins ready for action on the Western Front—did not possess a single automatic weapon. The French air service owned two machine guns, with no coherent plan for their use; the British also had two, and a sharp injunction from headquarters that under no circumstances were the heavy, hazardous weapons to be taken aloft.

"War? We had never seriously considered war," wrote a German Zeppelin commander; yet the first lethal assignment in the air war went to the dirigibles. Liége, ringed by a dozen forts, stood in the way of Moltke's rush across Belgium, and on August 6, 1914, the dirigible Z VI was ordered aloft to attack them. No flying ship in the German service had bona fide aerial bombs. Eight artillery shells, with fragments of horse blanket strapped on for fins, would have to do. They did not do much, and Belgian troops sent up such a barrage of ground fire that the Z VI, full of holes and leaking gas, barely managed to stagger back across the frontier for a crash-landing in a forest near Bonn.

Orders then went out for German airplanes to reconnoiter the forts —orders not too joyfully received at the commandeered pastures and other temporary sites where many of the German planes had collected in the War's first week. "Our airdrome at Montjoie was the worst place imaginable," wrote one airman. "Away to the south stretched great forests, to the east and west were steep cliffs." Despite the hazards of operating over strange and hostile terrain, however, the reconnaissance of the forts went off rather well. One observer scorned to settle for an aerial view. He ordered his pilot to land directly between two of the forts; then he looked them over at ground level and flew home to deliver what one proud German chronicler called "important reports to the high command." By mid-August Liége had fallen.

The dirigibles, however, continued to suffer. On August 21, two of Germany's three remaining frontline Zeppelins were forced down, one by French ground fire, the other at the hands of German troops who misunderstood its flare-gun recognition signals. Shortly thereafter French infantrymen put 1,300 bullet holes into one of their own dirigibles, two shell holes into another and forced down a third with more bullets. The French army's exasperated General Joseph Joffre ordered that henceforth no dirigibles of any kind were to be fired upon, but confidence in these great machines had gone down with the airships themselves. With the War barely started, all frontline air activity quickly shifted to the airplane sections.

The results at first were not auspicious. German aircraft sent over western and central Belgium toward the end of the second week of August failed to note the landing of 80,000 men and 30,000 horses of the British Expeditionary Force. One of the aviators, Lieutenant Reinhold Jahnow, crashed at Malmédy, a victim either of ground fire or plane malfunction; he is believed to have been the first German airman to die in action. In fact the chief danger to the airmen of either side in these early weeks continued to come from the ground. The planes remained unarmed except for a smattering of swords, pistols and carbines that were prescribed by traditional cavalry regulations but often left behind to save weight and to reduce clutter in the already constricted cockpits. No aviator had yet fired at another. On the day that Jahnow died, a French Morane-Saulnier and a German Taube crossed paths above the lines. The enemy fliers exchanged cordial waves and went their separate ways.

Despite such immunity from air attack, the quality of reconnaissance did not immediately improve. The French, who believed Moltke's smash on the north was but a feint, had positioned only a handful of planes opposite his front, and they failed to detect fully half of the 16 German corps and five cavalry divisions that were grinding across Belgium. In Lorraine to the east, where Joffre expected the heaviest German blow to fall and where France planned an offensive of its own, greater numbers of French planes failed to spot deep and bristling German defensive concentrations. A few troop sightings that turned out to be tar patches on roadways and a report of enemy tents that proved to be gravestone shadows did little to build the confidence of senior officers in aerial scouting.

At this moment Britain's airmen began to arrive on the Continent. For the Channel flight from Dover, the Royal Flying Corps had equipped its aviators with automobile-tire inner tubes to carry along as life preservers. These, together with field kits of canned bully beef, water bottles, chocolate bars and small stoves, had been carried to the debarkation field in requisitioned civilian delivery trucks still emblazoned with the names of their owners: Lazenby's Sauce, Peek Frean's Biscuits, and an outsized red van with "Bovril" in large black letters. One by one the loaded aircraft rose into the gusty Channel weather, with orders to "ram on sight" any Zeppelins encountered on the way.

None were, but one plane became diverted when the pilot puckishly tried to drop his inflated inner tube like a quoit onto the top of the lighthouse at Cap Gris-Nez. Another flier crash-landed near Boulogne in his unmarked plane and was promptly locked up by the French. Still other airmen spent that night in the plush Hôtel du Rhin in Amiens. The obliging proprietor passed out nightgowns to the airmen, whose kits did not include pajamas, and was treated to the sight of a six-foot-four-inch officer in a very attenuated nightgown dancing the cancan in the hotel corridors.

Almost at once the RFC moved to an airfield at Maubeuge to commence reconnaissance. The first report on August 19 read in part:

"Did not pick up my position on the map. Arrived at a big town, but could not place it on map. On my return I discovered this to have been Brussels." Though the French had adopted a red, white and blue roundel to distinguish their aircraft, the British still carried no markings beyond an occasional Union Jack flag sewed or painted on by the fliers. The British soon encountered what one man described as a "nasty habit" by friendly ground troops of "firing at every aeroplane they saw." Another pilot recorded his dismay at the arrival of the British infantry "because up till that moment we had only been fired on by the French. Now we were fired on by French *and* English."

Air reconnaissance—or lack of it—soon became a critical factor in the momentous ground battles of 1914. During the third week in August, the French army, blindly charging along a front from Lorraine to Mons, suffered 140,000 casualties in four days. And the British Expeditionary Force, equally blind, was unknowingly in danger of being annihilated altogether. Then, on August 23, Captain—later Air Chief Marshal—Philip Joubert, patrolling above the BEF's left flank near Mons, saw roads covered by "grey streams" of men "where we knew that there were no Allied troops."

Joubert had spotted the German II Corps sweeping around toward the British rear. A bullet rattled off the experimental steel plate under his seat and another pierced one side of his gas tank, but Joubert covered the hole with his fingers and managed to make it safely home. His report, supported by those of two other airmen, generated an instant order of withdrawal: "We move in four hours!" Had the airmen not made this crucial discovery, the Germans might indeed have been home by Christmas. As it was, the British barely escaped a major disaster. A young lieutenant wrote, "The Germans have us on the run and we are fighting a rearguard action against big odds. Men, guns and transport block all the roads. Men are throwing away their kits. Some carry their wounded pals and nearly all the carts and limbers have wounded in them."

Moving out at dusk in a pelting rain, the RFC spent the following week in headlong retreat, sleeping, one diarist noted, "as best we could. One night bivouacked under a hedge in a thunderstorm, the next in a very recently evacuated girls' school, and the next in the most modern hotel."

The airmen saved their planes, too, as best they could, flying them in and out of grainfields where the landing strips were marked either by small red flags that the men carried with them or by sheaves of wheat stacked in rows. Other sheaves were heaped up at night as wind buffers for the machines and as bedding for the men. The crew of one damaged plane took off its wings and tried to tow the fuselage down the road with a French motorcar they had requisitioned. Unfortunately the aircraft fell into a ditch. The men then destroyed what remained of the machine, stole bicycles and continued their retreat southward.

A pigeon is released from an RNAS seaplane to carry a message home. Before air-to-ground radios became standard equipment, pigeons often were used to transmit emergency messages that led to the rescue of dozens of downed fliers.

Under these trying conditions the Allied airmen ceased to feel quite so gentlemanly toward the Germans, particularly the ones who began to fly over their makeshift airdromes and harass them with small hand-tossed bombs. An exasperated Briton who "went up to have a go at one of these disturbers of our peace" managed to fire 30 rounds of ammunition at him from his revolver, entirely without effect. The Englishman then "landed in desperation and tied a hand grenade onto the end of a long piece of control cable with the bright idea of flying over the Hun and hitting his propeller with the grenade." But the Germans remained unscathed.

The French, too, were now trying to attack in the air. Besides their pistols and carbines, they took up grenades, an occasional shotgun, and even steel arrows called fléchettes, developed for use against ground troops, which they tried to dump down on enemy aircraft—all without effect. The German fliers remained under orders to stick to observation patrols and random bombing with hand missiles, but a French pilot

Back from a mission, French airmen busily write reconnaissance reports in a tent at Luneville, France. Their accounts of enemy troop dispositions and movements were digested, plotted on large maps and circulated in official dispatches.

returning with a hole in his plane complained, though it was never confirmed, that a German had thrown a brick at him.

The War was being waged with far more effect on the ground. In a month France had suffered half a million casualties, and Germans occupied one fourth of her territory. Moltke's scythe-cut through the coastal plain toward the rear of Paris moved relentlessly forward until German infantrymen at the point of the thrust, near the River Marne, could see the tip of the Eiffel Tower just 25 miles away. General Joffre told his troops to "die on the spot rather than surrender ground," and the civilian heads of the French Third Republic fled to Bordeaux. German planes began to enliven their reconnaissance missions by flying over Paris itself, dropping bombs and an occasional message of warning: "The German Army is at the gates of Paris. There is nothing for you to do but surrender." The planes came with such regularity in late afternoon that Parisians began to call the hour "Five o'clock Taube time." They turned out by the thousands to watch through opera glasses and

Flying low, a German seaplane patrols the barbed-wire-fortified beach at Ostend in Belgium. Germany took Ostend in 1914 and for a time its bombers fanned out from there to raid Allied cities. But the beach remained popular with civilian bathers.

even to sell seats at vantage points—despite the fact that the planes' bombs killed five people.

Then, after September 2, the planes stopped coming. So did the rest of Germany's forces. Moltke had decided not to send one of his armies behind Paris as planned but to turn it eastward along the Marne. For several days French and British aviators had been bringing home a jumble of reports indicating that such a move was under way. But nothing seemed clear, and by 8 p.m. on September 3, General Joseph-Simon Galliéni, the beleaguered military governor of Paris, erupted into a tirade against his largely inexperienced fliers. Their reports, he exploded, "amounted to almost nothing!" At just that moment a French plane brought in a new report, shortly confirmed by the British, that German forces were indeed "gliding from west to east," exposing themselves to a flank attack.

"We will fall on the back of their neck," said Galliéni, suddenly very calm. General Joffre confirmed the decision with his historic pronouncement, "Gentlemen, we will fight on the Marne." The Allies attacked with everything they could scrape together, and a serious gap appeared in the German front, threatening to cut off its westernmost wing. This time German reconnaissance fliers helped to avert disaster by spotting British units pressing into the hole. Warned, the Germans closed ranks.

But Paris had been saved. To the north the rival armies commenced a race to the sea in one last futile effort to outflank each other. Both sides dug in, and lines of trenches that would barely move throughout the rest of the War began to cut into the soil all the way to Switzerland.

In the confusion of the fast-changing situation on the ground, airmen of both sides again found themselves living off the open countryside. They bivouacked in haystacks, under the wings of their planes or in lean-to shelters made of broken airplane sections. They foraged for eggs and chickens, milked cows, shot rabbits and partridges, and cooked in cutoff petrol cans. As the fall weather deteriorated into wet, gusty storms, they pegged down their planes against the wind and the lucky ones crawled into barns to sleep, while others curled up under ponchos in their drenched cockpits.

They fought when and as they could. In one classic confrontation between the old chivalry and the new, a detachment of horsemen actually charged against a squadron of aircraft. A farmer in the Aisne River district northeast of Paris had informed the French cavalry that German planes had landed nearby. At 3 a.m. the cavalrymen, approaching the landing field as quietly as possible, drew their sabers and charged. A German machine gun mounted on a guardian automobile cut down 12 of the attacking horsemen, but the rest managed to destroy a number of the airplanes.

As the cavalry charge was a symbol of the past, another event along the Aisne held great portent for the future. A few British planes struggled aloft carrying 75-pound Morse-code radio transmitters. In late afternoon of September 24 one of them sent down what may have been air warfare's first radio-guided fire-control instructions:

4:02 p.m. A very little short. Fire. Fire.

4:12 p.m. A little short; line okay.

4:20 p.m. You were just between two batteries. Search 200 yards each side of your last shot. Range okay.

4:22 p.m. You have them.

4:26 p.m. Hit. Hit. Hit.

4:42 p.m. I am coming home now.

At almost the same time, other British air units mounted the first air raids on German soil. Planes of the Royal Naval Air Service had been sent to Dunkirk with instructions from First Lord of the Admiralty Winston Churchill to "deny the use of territory within 100 miles" of the city to German dirigibles and airplanes. The RNAS planes were hampered at first by bad weather and a lack of adequate terrain maps. When in late September they received the momentous order to go against the airship hangars at Düsseldorf and Cologne, four planes wandered around in a deep fog and returned disappointed; one pilot complained that "looking for the sheds at Düsseldorf was like going into a dark room to look for a black cat."

Then, on October 8, while one RNAS pilot dropped a pair of 20-pound bombs onto the Cologne railroad station, killing three civilians, another aviator found the cat. Flying a new biplane, the Sopwith Tabloid, with bombs hung from release racks under the fuselage, Lieutenant R. L. G. Marix came in at 600 feet over a hangar in Düsseldorf. His bombs fell precisely onto the target, transforming Germany's last frontline Zeppelin into an enormous torch of flaming hydrogen.

The British planned to launch their next raid from the farthest end of France. They disassembled four 80-horsepower Avro biplanes, packed them into unmarked trucks and, to avoid notice by German spies, drove by night to Belfort near the Swiss border. The target was Germany's main Zeppelin base at Friedrichshafen on the northern shore of Lake Constance. At noon on November 21 the reassembled planes skimmed in at 10 feet above the water, climbed to altitude and released 11 bombs that generated a gratifying pillar of flame. Later it turned out the fire came from a gas plant; the damage was repaired within a week. Both Zeppelins survived the strike. However, one British pilot very nearly did not. Shot down into a lakeside clearing, he was mauled by a group of furious civilians before being turned over to German soldiers. That evening, German officers toasted the bandaged Briton, raising their glasses to their "comrade of the skies."

Over the following month French Voisin biplanes twice attacked the railway station at Freiburg. The Germans, who had bombed Antwerp before capturing it in October, now assembled their most promising fliers into a special bombing unit at Ostend, on the occupied Channel coast. Code-named the Carrier Pigeons, they were to terrorize the British coast with raids. Actually they did not manage an attack for some months, although a plane from another unit did bomb Dover on December 21 and again on Christmas Eve. Ultimately, the Ostend group's most important service was to provide training for several young fliers whose exploits would soon be known around the world.

As 1914 ended, no true fighter plane had yet appeared over the trenches, and no ace or knight had yet been singled out for adulation. Yet in those few months, every major aspect of air warfare had at least been tried, including one that would indelibly define the nature of combat in the sky. On October 5, a French corporal named Louis Quénault was flying as observer in a rear-engined Voisin piloted by Sergeant Joseph Frantz. Quénault sat in front, his hands on a Hotchkiss machine gun newly fitted to the edge of the cockpit. Over Rheims the Frenchmen spotted a German Aviatik two-seater. Sergeant Frantz swung the Voisin into a headlong attack. The Germans seemed to be unconcerned as the French closed in. Then Quénault's Hotchkiss shuddered to life—and the German plane plunged to earth in flames, the first airplane to be shot down by a machine gun in aerial combat. 〰️

The moment of Corporal Louis Quénault's victory over a German Aviatik, the first air-to-air kill with a machine gun, is dramatized in this 1914 illustration for a popular magazine in still-neutral Italy. Actually, the French aircraft was a Voisin biplane, not the monoplane shown here.

Uniforms tailored in tradition

The airmen of World War I dressed in an array of garments that reflected both the older services from which many of them came and the new element in which they fought. Their outfits ranged from specialized gear that guarded them against the weather *(pages 42-43)* to standard service uniforms, worn on the ground and under protective clothing in flight.

The typical air officer purchased his service uniform, consisting of cap, tunic and trousers, from a tailor. Enlisted men generally were issued their outfits by the government. If an airman had transferred from another branch, he usually kept the uniform of his old unit, with aviation insignia added. The gold-braided Austro-Hungarian aviator's tunic at center below, for example, was adapted from the uniform of its owner's original unit—the Imperial and Royal Hussars—by adding gold balloons to the collar.

The colors of an airman's uniform ranged from flamboyant to drab, depending on the nation he served. Some French officers retained their traditional scarlet trousers and tunics of horizon blue *(opposite page)* even though the bright colors violated every principle of camouflage. The United States Air Service uniform, a muted olive, lacked both color and comfort. American airmen frequently complained that the rigid collars of their field tunics irritated their necks when they had to turn their heads quickly. Many discarded these confining coats and had local tailors make them new ones with comfortable open collars, like those worn by Britain's Royal Flying Corps.

GERMAN AIRMAN'S CAP AND TUNIC

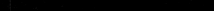

AUSTRO-HUNGARIAN KEPI AND TUNIC

HAT AND TUNIC OF GERMAN IN OTTOMAN AIR FORCE

FRENCH AIR MAJOR'S SERVICE DRESS

RFC CAPTAIN'S FIELD UNIFORM

ITALIAN AVIATOR'S TUNIC AND HAT

U.S. AIR SERVICE UNIFORM

Suiting up against the elements

Cold, wind, rain, glare and spewing engine oil were formidable foes for the open-cockpit aviator. To protect themselves, airmen took to the skies wearing all manner of goggles, leather coats and helmets, fur-lined boots and gloves.

Basic flight clothing, much of it patterned after the wardrobes of seamen and early motorists, was issued to all fliers. But most airmen supplemented their regulation apparel with layers of warmer, specialized garments that they bought themselves, received in packages from home or took from captured enemy pilots. Some fliers even stuffed their flying clothes with newspaper, the time-tested insulation of the vagabond.

There were aviators, however, who disdained protective gear. British ace Albert Ball, for one, refused to wear either helmet or goggles because he felt that they impaired his vision.

GERMAN PILOT'S HELMET AND GOGGLES
These goggles, now cracked, protected the eyes but reduced peripheral vision.

BRITISH AIRMAN'S LEATHER FLYING HELMET
The owner decorated this cap with a button of the First Aid Nursing Yeomanry.

HEADGEAR OF AN RFC FLIER
Worn with goggles, this cold-weather gear completely covered an airman's face.

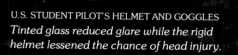
U.S. STUDENT PILOT'S HELMET AND GOGGLES
Tinted glass reduced glare while the rigid helmet lessened the chance of head injury.

AMERICAN FLYING CAP AND GOGGLES
Made of splinterproof glass, these tinted eye protectors were prized by U.S. fliers.

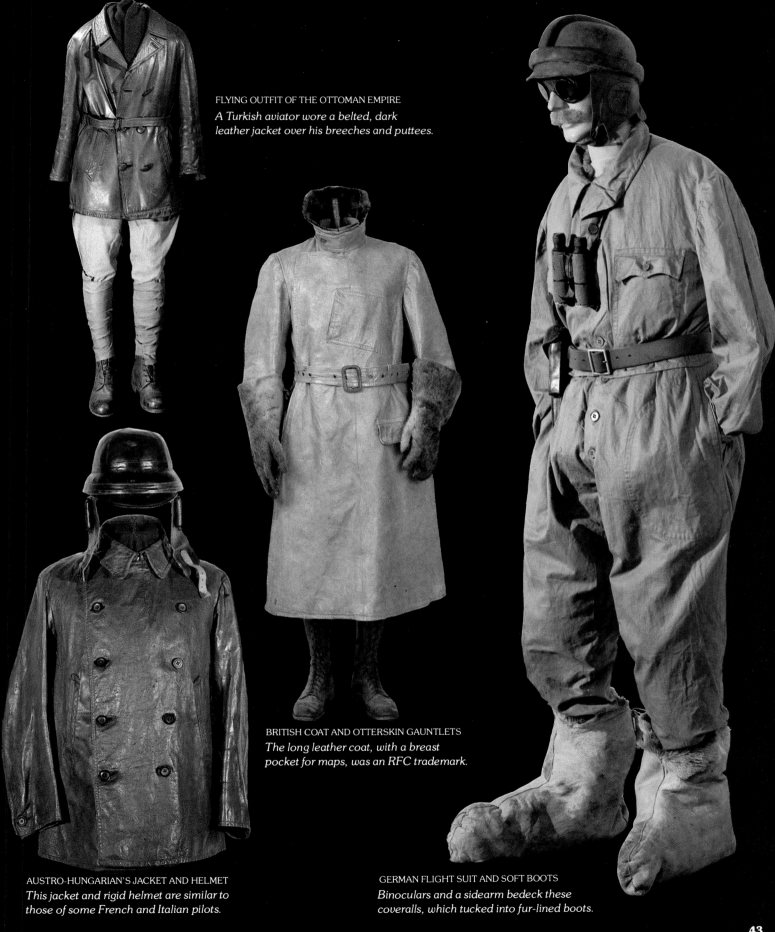

FLYING OUTFIT OF THE OTTOMAN EMPIRE
A Turkish aviator wore a belted, dark leather jacket over his breeches and puttees.

BRITISH COAT AND OTTERSKIN GAUNTLETS
The long leather coat, with a breast pocket for maps, was an RFC trademark.

AUSTRO-HUNGARIAN'S JACKET AND HELMET
This jacket and rigid helmet are similar to those of some French and Italian pilots.

GERMAN FLIGHT SUIT AND SOFT BOOTS
Binoculars and a sidearm bedeck these coveralls, which tucked into fur-lined boots.

2

In pursuit of the Blue Max

Stalemated on the ground, the belligerent nations in 1915 began for the first time to look to the air for an edge in what promised to be a grueling war of attrition. As the military grew increasingly confident in the airmen, the sporadic flights of the War's early months gave way to regular assignments for reconnaissance and artillery spotting. Officers with some understanding of the potential of air power came to the fore, and a new generation of aircraft, still rudimentary but designed with the needs of combat in mind, began to appear on the Western Front.

Most significantly, the planes were better armed—chiefly with weapons intended to drive one another from the sky. By the end of the first full year of war, the machine gun had forever replaced the carbine and the brick. The French, so often pioneers in matters of aviation, found a way to shoot machine-gun bullets through a moving propeller—whereupon the Germans developed a better system. For a time German planes became the scourge of the air.

The aviators found this swift escalation in the importance, and deadliness, of their role both exciting and perilous. Even the best of them were still learning to cope with balky weapons and unpredictable flying machines, both old and new, in an environment that became more lethal by the week.

For the fliers, the year started slowly. The winter of 1915 was one of the worst in years and few Allied or German airmen found it possible to stay warm, or dry—or even airborne—for long in the bitter, snowy storms. A young British observer described gales so strong in northern France that "when we tried to fly into the teeth of the wind, we found ourselves standing still." A single storm wrecked 30 planes of the Royal Flying Corps on the ground. Georges Guynemer, accepted for pilot training after he had completed his mechanic's apprenticeship, eagerly reported to his new assignment at the French airdrome at Pau—and was handed a snow shovel.

But soon improving weather would bring action enough. Men learned to work as teams with their planes, their comrades and their vital ground crews. And from the sometimes funny, sometimes fatal confusion, individual airmen emerged whose exploits as destroyers of enemy planes made them bona fide heroes—a commodity that was sorely needed and soon exploited by all the war-stunned nations. But first each of these knights-in-training had a great deal to learn.

The German Empire's preeminent state, Prussia, bestowed its highest military honor, membership in the order Pour le Mérite, on 81 airmen during the War. Popularly known as the Blue Max, the medal bore a crowned F for Frederick the Great, who established the order in 1740. The medal was inscribed in French, which was then the language of the Prussian court.

More than one pilot developed a love-hate relationship with his plane. They were cranky, primitive machines, and although they seemed wonderful in their time (and, of course, were), they were hard to start, hard to fly, dangerous to maneuver.

Much of the difficulty undoubtedly lay in the newness of aviation itself, and the relative inexperience of the pilots. Much of it lay in the complexity of the simplest tasks, which often required four hands. Starting the engine, for example, was a tricky procedure involving a fairly intricate choreography between pilot and mechanic.

The pilot first would hand-pump air pressure into the gas tank, with the ignition switch off and both his air- and gas-intake valves open. Then, as the mechanic cranked the propeller by hand, the pilot slowly shut down his air valve. When the mechanic, standing next to the engine, had determined that the pistons had sucked in enough gas, he shouted "Contact!" and the pilot turned on the ignition. The mechanic gave the propeller a final heave and jumped back for his life; assuming all was well, the engine coughed and started.

Taking off, the pilot was on his own, and for a green pilot in a 1915 plane, the experience could be harrowing. The American volunteer Victor Chapman, who had transferred out of the Foreign Legion and into the French air service, described one of his early takeoffs in a stiff breeze: "The machine left the ground almost immediately, and I had to hold it down to keep headway. Then it began to buck, squirm and wriggle. It slid off to the right, to the left, took a short plunge downward and then attempted to rear. The earth, a scrawny tree or two, looked near and menacing." Needless to say, Chapman made it into the air.

Trees or no, a pilot had to remember not to turn too soon after takeoff, lest the plane lose air speed, stall and crash. Because of gyroscopic force, a plane with a rotary engine tended to nose down on a right-hand turn and up on a left-hand turn—which made right turns close to the ground especially dangerous. Unless the pilot applied a large degree of opposite rudder, the plane might crash.

Once aloft, a pilot faced other hazards, some merely irritating, others potentially fatal. There was the nauseating vapor of burned castor-oil lubricant, and gas fumes so strong that a man might pass out if he did not occasionally breathe the fresh air from the slip stream. Leaks in the plane's fuel system might send gasoline spilling onto a hot engine. ("Fire," said the pilot of a two-seater, "was our third passenger.")

The hazards were too much for many young fliers, and accidents continued to account for up to half of all fatalities. The log of one Belgian air unit for one three-week period was a litany of noncombat disasters: "Piret sideslipped to the ground"; "de Catillon turned upside down"; "Vergult smashed up"; "Adrien Richard capsized."

Following aviation's vital reconnaissance work at the Marne, General Joffre, filled with a new respect for planes, put an experienced pilot, Major Edouard Barès, in command of the French air service. Barès had

Bemedaled ace Max Immelmann restrains his pet dog Tyras in 1916. As one of Germany's first air heroes, Immelmann was formally made a knight of five different orders including the Pour le Mérite.

received his first taste of air combat as a volunteer in the Balkan Wars of 1912-1913, and he quickly proved to be an efficient leader. He brought the aerial observers under his command, centralized the French photo reconnaissance units, scavenged the French Army for mechanics, and reorganized the air service into three specialized groups, for bombing, fighting, and reconnaissance and artillery spotting. Each group was divided into escadrilles of three to six planes.

Barès also got a flow of better airplanes moving toward the front. Improved models began to replace the oldest Voisins, which one pilot had described as "a sort of nightmare in which the staid four-poster canopy bed takes to flying." The Henry Farmans, with their engines located aft just below the fuel tank, also were being weeded out, to the regret of at least one German flier who had noted with satisfaction, "They catch fire so easily." Increasing numbers of sturdy twin-engined Caudrons appeared, ungainly-looking craft but airworthy enough to be used into 1917—though one young pilot complained that an early model had "the gliding angle of a brick" (it would become a standard complaint of pilots about airplanes they did not like). Soon a new two-seater, the Nieuport 10, arrived, and the manufacturer already was experimenting with its successor, the Nieuport 11 *"Bébé,"* a wonderfully quick little single-seated biplane that could carry a machine gun mounted on its upper wing to fire forward above the propeller.

Major Barès had ordered a supply of Hotchkiss machine guns and by February 1915 some 50 of them had arrived—too few to arm more than a fraction of the 390 French planes deployed along the front, but enough to thoroughly frighten the Germans. As with every new weapon, when it appeared in a few places it was reported to be everywhere. In June a fledgling German pilot, Max Immelmann, wrote home that it was "impossible to fly across the lines" because the French were so well armed. Of one mission he wrote: "Suddenly I heard the familiar tack-tack-tack of the machine guns and saw little holes appearing in our right wing. It is a horrible feeling to have to wait until one is perhaps hit, without being able to fire a shot oneself."

The Germans still flew with no weapons except pistols and carbines, as in fact did most of the Allies. On February 5 France's Adolphe Pégoud, a redoubtable prewar civilian pilot, took on two German planes in plain sight of the trenches. Maneuvering with dazzling skill, he kept his Morane Parasol so close to the Germans that his observer dispatched them both with six rifle shots.

The British in early spring at last officially permitted the mounting of a Lewis gun at the rear of the observer's seat in twin-cockpit planes. But there were as yet no machine-gun virtuosos in the RFC. Lieutenant Sholto Douglas, who one day, in another war, would command all of Great Britain's fighter planes, described his first effort to shoot down another plane: "Facing backward, I started blazing away . . . but the enemy merely turned away quite unharmed and went about his business." Douglas' experience was typical. Many airmen had never even

Crewmen manuever an Italian dirigible out of its hangar. The cameras slung under the gondola provided overlapping visual fields.

A revealing "war of lenses"

The camera quickly became such a valuable tool for airborne observers that one contemporary writer called World War I "a war of lenses." Photographs taken from airplanes, balloons and dirigibles and developed in frontline laboratories disclosed minute details of enemy positions and movements. A picture taken from 15,000 feet could be magnified to reveal the footprints of an infantryman.

Technicians pieced the pictures together to form mosaic maps of the battle zones. Eventually one immense photographic map, in thousands of sections, showed the entire Western Front.

A British photographer tests a camera mounted near the nose of an F.E.2b pusher biplane.

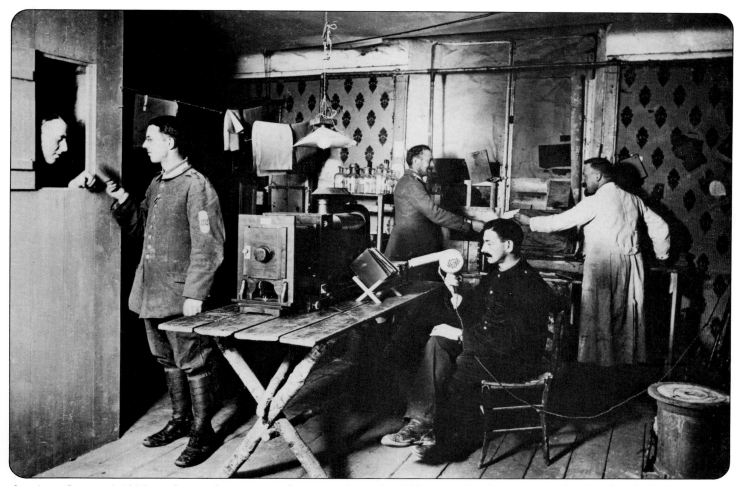

In a busy German field lab, a photo technician, seated, uses an electric hand blower to dry glass negatives developed in the darkroom at left.

With individual exposures pinned into place on his worktable, a British photo-technician (left) creates a composite map. Above, Canadian ace Frederick McCall studies an aerial photograph before going on a mission. In the last two years of the War, the British alone took more than 500,000 reconnaissance photos.

fired a machine gun until they tried to hit another aircraft with one.

The weapons themselves were awkward appendages. The first gun mounts were crude side-cockpit brackets made of steel tubing from which, in the midst of combat, the gun sometimes worked loose and fell overboard. The earliest guns held 50 rounds or less, so that they often emptied in one or two brief bursts. Reloading in a bucking, swooping aircraft was hard enough for an observer wearing clumsy flight gloves or working with bare, numbed fingers. For a man flying alone it was a gymnastic feat. Holding the stick control with his legs, the pilot had to reach for the drum, release it and replace it; all during this time the enemy was either trying to kill him or escape.

One of the most frightening adventures any flier ever survived unharmed befell the RFC's Louis Strange when he tried to reload while in combat over Belgium. He was trying to detach an empty and balky drum, Strange related later, with the stick between his knees, when he raised himself in his seat to get a better grip. At that moment the plane stalled and flicked over into a spin. Strange was thrown out of the cockpit, but he managed to keep both hands on the drum of the Lewis gun. "Only a few seconds previously I had been cursing because I could not get that drum off," he wrote. "Now I prayed fervently that it would stay on forever."

Strange's chin was rammed against the top wing while his legs waved about in empty air. "It dawned on me," he wrote, "that my only chance of righting the machine lay in getting my feet into the cockpit. I kept on kicking upwards behind me until I got first one foot and then the other hooked inside. Somehow I got the stick between my legs again and jammed on full aileron and elevator. The machine came over the right way up, and I fell into my seat with a bump."

The skill and the numbers of Allied gunners and guns continued to increase and the Germans were becoming more and more concerned. By midwinter Germany had yet to score an official air-to-air kill, though unconfirmed claims indicated at least one plane downed. When Allied aircraft appeared, "the best means of defense," according to young Immelmann, "was a speedy retreat." One result was that German ground forces rarely saw a friendly plane. The men at the front began to grumble, not only at the lack of artillery spotting and field reconnaissance but at the too-frequent appearance of Allied planes overhead, particularly in late afternoon, when the obscuring glare of the setting sun favored aircraft coming from the west.

During German infantry attacks at Soissons and Allied offensives in Champagne and at Neuve-Chapelle in the early months of 1915, the Germans received virtually no information or other help from their aircraft. Allied planes carried out superb photo-reconnaissance—a vital factor now that the antagonists were frozen into trench positions of almost indescribable intricacy. At Neuve-Chapelle, systematic flights gave British generals an unprecedented look at every detail of the German positions for a depth of 700 to 1,500 yards along their entire front.

After Allied planes had photographed the rail center of Courtrai in German-held Belgium, three bombs caused 75 casualties and tied up railroad traffic for three days. All along the front, Allied reconnaissance planes would swoop just above the trenches before an infantry attack to see whether their artillery had cut the German barbed wire. One British pilot, Lanoe Hawker, found a precarious but effective way to locate camouflaged enemy guns: "I fly low and draw their fire," he said, "then mark it down on the map." On one such sortie Hawker picked up 50 bullet holes in his plane and one in his leg.

Although Allied airmen at this time had little to fear from German planes, the persistent shelling by German antiaircraft guns was a great source of anxiety. "I notice several people's nerves are not as strong as they used to be," an RFC diarist noted, "and I am sure Archie is responsible." Even the otherwise nerveless Hawker reported in some anger that "apparently one of the great amusements of the fellows in the trenches is watching our aeroplanes being shelled, and a lot of betting

Frenchman Roland Garros, the first flier to score a victory by firing through a propeller, stands above the wire-braced wing of a prewar Morane-Saulnier monoplane. Captured in 1915, Garros escaped but later was killed in action.

results.'' In March one close shellburst left Hawker with a concussion and a two-week headache. The German gunners would have been delighted to know they were that effective. Their own reports estimated that barely half of their antiaircraft shells exploded, scoring hits on but 30 of 600 intended targets.

The Germans were not only outgunned, they were outnumbered— with some 230 frontline aircraft to the Allies' 500—and on April 1, 1915, their situation took a turn for the worse. On that day Adolphe Pégoud scored his third victory, more than any other pilot in the world up to then; Jean Navarre, who would become one of France's most colorful aces, scored his first. And, from an airfield near Dunkirk, French Lieutenant Roland Garros took off armed with a device that for a time would make his plane the most feared weapon in the air.

Before the War Garros had won acclaim at international air meets, had set an altitude record of more than 18,000 feet and—in 1913— had become the first man to fly across the Mediterranean. But his first efforts as a combat pilot had netted him nothing. "I was able to outmaneuver my adversary," Garros wrote, "but my observer never succeeded in shooting him down with the light rifle, carbine or shotgun that constituted our armament."

On a visit to Paris, Garros expressed his frustration to Raymond Saulnier, the plane builder. In April of 1914 Saulnier had applied for a patent on a cam-operated mechanism that, in theory at least, would enable a machine gun to fire cleanly between the blades of a revolving propeller. The design was sound enough. Unfortunately, the available Hotchkiss machine gun tended to fire at an uneven rate and the ammunition it used produced a high proportion of delayed "hang-fire" rounds. No device could keep it from mistiming and shooting up the wooden propeller. But Saulnier also showed Garros something else he had designed: a steel deflector that, when fastened to the propeller, would protect it from damage by the small percentage of bullets that might actually hit it. Intrigued, Garros and another friend, master mechanic Jules Hue, set to work to test the deflector idea. They bolted a gun and engine onto an obsolete plane. "I started the engine," wrote Hue. "Garros fired . . . and everything collapsed. The engine fell to the ground, one blade of the airscrew having flown off, and the fuselage broke behind the cockpit. What had happened? One of the braces holding the deflectors had broken."

Hue thereupon fashioned better braces and produced a more streamlined set of deflectors: wedge shaped, with gutter-like channels for the bullets. In March Garros reappeared at St.-Pol airdrome near Dunkirk with a Hotchkiss gun on a fixed mount behind the shielded propeller of a Morane-Saulnier monoplane, and on April 1 he took off alone toward the German lines.

Officially, his mission was to bomb the railroad station at nearby Ostend. But along came a German Albatros, seeking a look at the Allied

Early implements of death from the air

The weapons of ground warfare quickly found their way into the air. At first pilots exchanged potshots—usually wildly inaccurate—with one another, using side arms, rifles and shotguns. From above an enemy they sometimes dropped grenades, and on occasion a flier trailed a long, weighted cable in the hope that it would tangle the other fellow's propeller.

For aerial attacks on infantry and cavalry, the French set great store in pencil-sized steel darts called fléchettes *(right)*. The needle-sharp missiles were carried in canisters slung under the fuselage and were released by a trigger located in the cockpit. Dropped from an altitude of 1,500 feet, a fléchette could go completely through the body of a horse. But such primitive aerial arms soon gave way to far deadlier weapons *(overleaf)*.

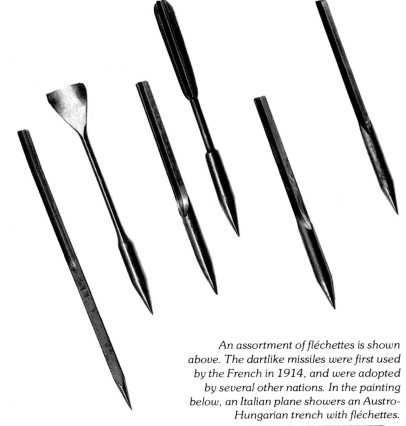

An assortment of fléchettes is shown above. The dartlike missiles were first used by the French in 1914, and were adopted by several other nations. In the painting below, an Italian plane showers an Austro-Hungarian trench with fléchettes.

An arsenal of fast-firing killers

In the air, as in the trenches, the machine gun became the War's deadliest weapon. Five of the guns most widely used on aircraft are shown here with their nations of manufacture.

The lightweight, reliable Lewis .303-caliber gun was designed by an American but was produced primarily in Great Britain. The Hotchkiss, fed ammunition from a belt or a 25-shot metal tray, was used successfully early in the War, but it proved hard to reload in flight and was relegated to the trenches.

The Allies' premier machine gun was the Vickers. It fired 800 rounds per minute and, when teamed with the Constantinesco hydraulic synchronizer, became the most lethal weapon in the air.

Germany's LMG.08/15, which was commonly called the Spandau after the town of its manufacture, was rigged to the early Fokker synchronizing gear and became the primary fixed, forward-firing gun on German fighters. The air-cooled Parabellum, so called for the code name of its manufacturer, was most often used by the observer in a two-seater, who fired it from a flexible mount.

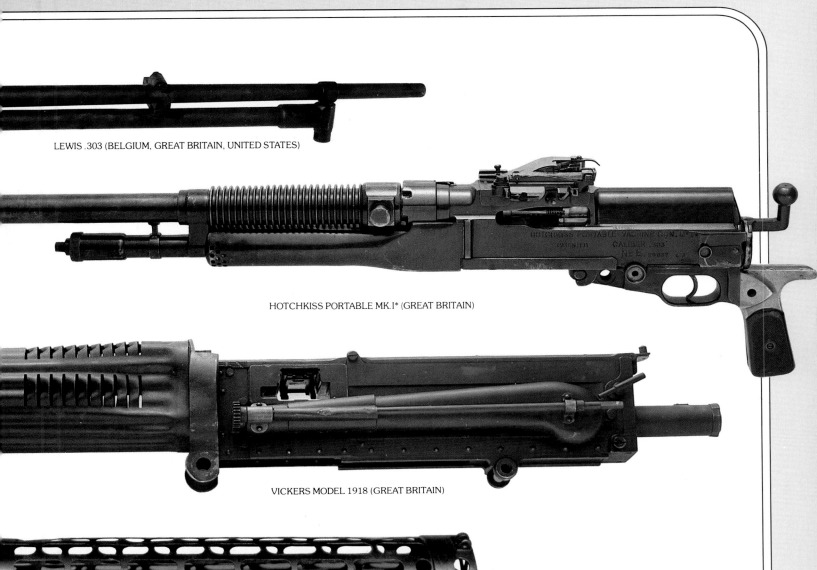

LEWIS .303 (BELGIUM, GREAT BRITAIN, UNITED STATES)

HOTCHKISS PORTABLE MK. I* (GREAT BRITAIN)

VICKERS MODEL 1918 (GREAT BRITAIN)

LMG.08/15 SPANDAU (GERMANY)

PARABELLUM MG.13 (GERMANY)

trenches after a week of bad weather. Garros, climbing, bore in on the German plane. Then, from just behind his propeller came the orange winking, the thin smoke trail, the noisy rattle of a machine gun. The surprised Germans fired back with a carbine, but it was no contest. Garros furiously slammed fresh ammunition into the gun until, on the third clip, "an immense flame burst out of the German motor and spread instantly." The Albatros went into a wide spiral and crashed. "I gazed below me for a long time," Garros wrote later, "to convince myself that it was not a nightmare."

Never before had a man aimed his entire plane as though it were the weapon, and shot through the propeller to bring down an enemy. The deflectors might be jury-rigged and imperfect, but they had worked, and the portent for the future was incalculable. On April 15 Garros, again firing through the shielded propeller, shot down a second German plane. Early in the morning of April 18 he got his third, making him second only to Pégoud, with five.

But later that very day Garros trumped himself. In the afternoon he again took off from Dunkirk, swooped too low behind the enemy lines and had his gas line cut by a single bullet fired from the ground. After gliding to earth, he tried to set fire to his plane to protect the secret of its armament. But he was too slow. German troops captured the plane, and Garros, intact.

The Germans were jubilant over the opportunity to unravel the mystery of the French plane that had destroyed three of theirs in less than three weeks. Ironically, the technology needed to develop an even more sophisticated method of shooting through the propeller was already available to them. Franz Schneider, a Swiss engineer working in Berlin, had applied for a patent on a synchronizing device even before Saulnier had; unlike the French, the Germans had an air-cooled Parabellum machine gun that was reliable enough to be adapted to the timing mechanism. But Schneider had been given no machine guns to work with. Instead, once Garros and his plane were in their hands, German authorities assigned another engineer to develop an imitation of the captured French device. Meanwhile, Allied airmen continued to dominate the sky.

French fliers who had received deflector-equipped Moranes flew behind the German lines, shooting down obsolescent Albatroses and slow-moving L.V.G.s, whose water-cooled engines spewed steam and scalding water when hit. In late May, 17 French bombers dropped 87 bombs in a dawn raid on the poison-gas works at Ludwigshafen in retaliation for Germany's first use of that hideous weapon during an assault on Ypres a few weeks before.

During a British raid on Courtrai on April 26, Lieutenant W. B. Rhodes-Moorhouse earned the first Victoria Cross awarded to an aviator. Rhodes-Moorhouse flew in low over the target to drop his bomb despite enemy ground fire that tore into his thigh, ripped his abdomen and creased his hand. Fighting dizziness and loss of blood, he got

The first German bomb to land on London was an incendiary dropped from a Zeppelin on May 31, 1915. Its shell (top) survived intact, though it crashed into a house and set two rooms on fire. The destruction wrought by dirigibles was not great—557 Britons died in airship raids—but the huge, silent bombers inspired such terror that the recruiting poster above actually exploited the home-front panic.

back to his base and reported before sinking into unconsciousness, and eventual death.

The next two Victoria Crosses for airmen came soon after. As part of the world's first strategic bombing plan, the Germans in late May had sent Zeppelins to bomb London. Though the great silver ships, troubled more by wind and fog than by any man-made defense, did little damage at first, they terrified the British.

On the night of June 6, the RNAS squadron on duty at Dunkirk received a dirigible alert. Sublieutenant Reginald Alexander John Warneford took off to intercept, and over Belgium he found the LZ 37 heading for England. Warneford climbed 150 feet above the airship and dropped his full load of bombs. The Zeppelin erupted in an enormous ball of flame. The explosion heaved Warneford's plane 200 feet straight up and onto its back, but the young aviator regained control in time to save himself and to glimpse the remains of the airship, "its pieces ablaze, strange and terrible torches, hundreds of them floating lazily to earth." For the first time, an airplane had brought down a dirigible, and Warneford's feat was acclaimed as an event of David and Goliath proportions. (Within the month he too would be down, killed in an accident while trying out a new plane.)

The other Victoria Cross went to Lanoe Hawker. Hawker had been flying in combat almost since the War began, and he was starved for a victory. His observer complained that, despite his own most earnest efforts with two machine guns swivel mounted on their F.E.2b, the impatient Hawker "had a foul habit of carrying an ordinary rifle which he used to loose off if he didn't think I was doing too well. The noise just over my head was most alarming."

Then, in June, Hawker wrote delightedly in his journal, "I have a beautiful little toy, a new Bristol Scout that goes at 80 m.p.h. and climbs 500 or 600 feet a minute. I'm having a machine gun fitted." Hawker had the gun bracketed next to the left side of the cockpit, jutting out obliquely and slightly downward, to miss the propeller. A week later he wrote, "I have badly frightened one or two Boches but have not yet had the luck to knock them out, I'm afraid. It's quite exciting diving at 120 m.p.h. firing a machine gun!"

On July 25, Hawker's luck changed. About 6 p.m. he spotted a pair of German biplanes and fired a burst at each from about 400 yards, forcing one of them to land. An hour later he saw another two-seater, and this time he stalked it like a hunter. Carefully he maneuvered his Bristol above the German, who apparently had not seen him, edging over until he could make his move from directly out of the setting sun. Then he dived at the unsuspecting German, gingerly pushing the rudder pedal until he was hurtling crabwise, with the machine gun lined up on the quarry. Hawker held fire until a collision seemed inevitable; then he cut loose and turned away. The German machine flipped into a fatal spin. On his return, Hawker was recommended for the first Victoria Cross ever awarded "for success in Air Combat."

The period of Allied superiority in the air was about to be rudely ended. Germany's air command had been industriously putting its house in order. The field forces were unified under an extraordinarily able officer, Lieutenant Colonel Hermann von der Lieth-Thomsen, and one of his first orders called for the arming of planes with Parabellum machine guns or Mauser automatic rifles. The weapons were mounted on rails, or on ring mounts encircling the observer's cockpit, giving him a wide field of fire without his having to manhandle the gun from one socket to another, or to worry about having it fall over the side.

By late spring Germany had fielded 74 sections of four to six planes each, the tactical equivalent of the French escadrille and the larger British squadron, which usually had 12 planes. Germany now had 17 flight schools, and waves of new pilots were arriving at the front with as many as 50 hours of flying time behind them. Perhaps most important, the Germans had turned over the challenge of imitating—or improving upon—the Garros-Saulnier machine-gun gear to a very clever and ambitious Dutchman who had immigrated to Germany before the War.

Anthony Fokker was one of the most fascinating, and controversial, young men in the young field of aviation. Not truly a designer—or an engineer or a combat pilot—he might best be called an inspired entrepreneur. Three things in life interested him: airplanes, money and Tony Fokker. And he did not hide his interests. He had learned the basics of aviation at a technical school near Mainz and soon was building airplanes of his own, working with a series of designer-partners with whom he usually parted on less than cordial terms. By 1913 he had established a successful flying school and a small aircraft works in Schwerin, about 100 miles northwest of Berlin. He was 24 when the War began; before it was over, planes bearing his name would symbolize the pinnacle of German air power.

"Imitator" was one label pinned on Fokker. He cheerfully admitted having been expelled from a hangar before the War while attempting to transcribe onto paper the design lines of a Morane-Saulnier, and then buying for junk in Paris a battered version of the plane, which he hauled home to finish copying. But Fokker at worst was a synthesizer; he had the intuition to sense what was needed in a new plane, the energy to ferret out the advances of others and the managerial skill to bring the parts together. The Fokker M.5 that grew out of the junked Morane was in several ways better than the French original: The wing had a superior airfoil, producing more lift, and the fuselage was of welded steel tubing instead of wood. The engine was worse: an 80 horsepower Oberursel—which was really a modified Gnome, produced under license from French blueprints, but which, unlike the French model, often overheated, causing frequent emergency landings.

Fokker was forthright about being a businessman interested chiefly in making a profit. "My mood was to say yes to everyone," he said, "and to sell to the first buyer who planked down his money on the barrel head." The German and Austro-Hungarian governments already had

Blazing fiercely, the hydrogen-filled German Zeppelin L Z 37 goes down over Belgium in this painting of the first air-to-air victory of a plane over a dirigible. On June 7, 1915, Sublieutenant R. A. J. Warneford of the RNAS flew his Morane monoplane over the length of the huge airship, dropping six bombs. For this mission Warneford won the Victoria Cross and the Légion d'Honneur.

Italy's romantic view of aerial war

When Italy entered the War in 1915, its Air Corps consisted of 86 planes and 72 pilots. But the Italians were boundlessly enthusiastic about aviation and were convinced of its military potential. They expressed their commitment by pouring large sums of money into aircraft production and, more romantically, by circulating artistic postcards like the ones shown here, which blended patriotic and aviation themes.

Such ardor paid dividends; Italy eventually developed an effective Air Corps consisting of 1,600 planes. It was supplemented by units from other Allied nations, including in 1917-1918 a United States contingent led by an American with Italian roots, Captain Fiorello H. La Guardia—a future mayor of New York.

Escorted by a mighty winged centaur and a maiden representing victory, two airplanes are shown cruising the heavens in this postcard distributed by the Italian Aeronautical Command.

On a postcard designed by the Italian sculptor Mastroianni, an aviator flying a plane with a warlike ram's head is led into battle by protective spirits.

Hovering over a battlefield, a winged goddess of victory bestows her blessings simultaneously on soldiers in the trenches below and airmen soaring above.

A personification of Italy exhorts her countrymen to conquer the disputed cities of Trieste and Trento with the patriotic rallying cry, "Onward, Savoy!"

invested enough money in Fokker's planes to turn his factory at Schwerin from a debt-ridden collection of little sheds into a going business. Then, in May of 1915, Lieutenant Colonel von der Lieth-Thomsen's adjutant came to him with an emergency proposition: Could he produce a forward-firing machine gun mounted on an airplane able to fly against the best made in France and Britain?

In later years Tony Fokker spun a glamorous tale about how he seized the invitation, raced back to Schwerin and, in 48 hours, almost single-handedly developed the world's first combat-ready synchronizer. The story was at least two parts nonsense, conjured up to enhance the reputation of the Fokker aircraft business and its owner.

What really happened at Schwerin was impressive enough. Fokker already had a first-rate new airplane, the fast, light and highly maneuverable M.5K, a few of which were in service as dispatch carriers. Now he huddled with his trusted assistants, Heinrich Luebbe and Fritz Heber, and tried to design a firing system for it. Whether they were already working on a synchronizer, and how much they knew of Franz Schneider's work in Germany and Raymond Saulnier's in France, is unclear. But together the Fokker team built a cam-operated push-rod control mechanism connecting it to the oil-pump drive of an Oberursel engine and the trigger of a Parabellum machine gun. They then attached a plywood disc to the Oberursel's propeller and kept test-firing until they got an even pattern of bullet holes between the blades. Finally they mounted the whole works on the Fokker M.5K and reported to Döberitz air base with the world's first reliable single-seated fighter plane. The operation had taken, not 48 hours, but several days of around-the-clock work.

Fokker, a superb exhibition pilot, demonstrated the synchronized gun at Döberitz. Then he took two prototypes of the new plane, now redesignated the E.I, to Douai in German-held France, where some of the best German pilots took turns crowding with him into the cockpit and going aloft to get the feel of the plane and the firing system. One man who quickly mastered both was Oswald Boelcke, a blond, good-natured and resourceful 23-year-old who was destined to become Germany's most respected fighter pilot and combat leader. Boelcke had already won an Iron Cross for carrying out more than 40 reconnaissance missions, and he had test-flown almost every make of plane in the German Air Service. He heartily approved of Fokker's synchronizing gear. He also liked the E.I's steadiness in a dive and the fact that the gun's trigger had been placed on the control stick so that a man could fly and shoot with one hand, rather than try to coordinate both hands in a simultaneous juggling of shooting and steering. Another fascinated onlooker at the Fokker demonstrations was Max Immelmann, who had joined Boelcke in Air Section 62 and was hungry for a machine that could give him his first kill.

The first Fokker E.Is were delivered to German frontline units by midsummer. Two of them were assigned to Boelcke and Immelmann. It was as though the two young pilots had been born to fly this airplane at this moment, when the conditions of battle demanded not only a superior plane but men with the right mentality to use it. Until now the emphasis in all the air services had been upon reconnaissance and, to a lesser extent, bombing. A flier's chief asset was not so much his ability to fight as to fly steadily and to identify enemy targets on the ground. Henceforth both sides would use fighters in increasing numbers to cut off the reconnaissance, to knock down bombers and to contend in a bitter war for supremacy of the air—just as Italy's Lieutenant Colonel Douhet and England's Captain Dickson had predicted they would before the War began. Fighting such a war required men with the instinct for combat and the sang-froid to go it alone.

Boelcke was such a man. "I believe in the saying that 'the strong man is mightiest alone,' " he wrote to his parents the week he got his Fokker. "I have attained my ideal with this single-seater. Now I can be pilot, observer and fighter all in one." Immelmann, like Boelcke, was both a natural athlete and a passionate flier who once wrote home that he was "drunk with joy" at becoming a student pilot. As a student he made 130 smooth landings—the number itself was a tribute to the thoroughness of German flight training—before he cracked up when his plane "got a nasty jolt from a heap of manure and turned over with me inside." But nothing could contain Immelmann's enthusiasm for flying. "A fall from 500 meters lasts 10 seconds," he wrote, "so that you have enough time to sing 'Heil Dir im Siegerkranz' and give three cheers for the Emperor" on the way down.

The personalities of Boelcke and Immelmann were as different as those of two comrades could be. Boelcke liked the ladies, courted a young French girl near Douai and once was censured for taking German nurses joy riding in the delicious squeeze of a Fokker's cockpit. Immelmann showed no interest in any woman but his mother, who faithfully sent him boxes of chocolates. Boelcke, though he thought of himself as a lone warrior, radiated leadership. While still a cadet he wrote, "You can win the men's confidence if you associate with them naturally and do not try to play the high and mighty superior."

Early on, Immelmann displayed a streak of petulance. One of his instructors, while conceding high marks for Immelmann's "youthful vigor and energy," noted that these qualities "were coupled with a truly childish temperament." Once he got near the front, however, Immelmann used all that energy.

The German Air Service, during the worst months of winter and spring, had ordered its outnumbered and underarmed pilots to fly only within their own lines; now that the E.I with its synchronizing gear had arrived, the high command became doubly adamant that the precious secret not be lost. Boelcke, however, had often ignored the directive, and Immelmann, following his example, became just as aggressive. The two men agreed on how the new Fokker planes should be used against the enemy. "One must not wait till they come across," wrote Boelcke,

The enterprising young Dutchman Tony Fokker (left) fostered close relationships with the German pilots who flew his planes. This postcard shows him with Lieutenant Kurt Wintgens, who is credited with the first unconfirmed victory in a Fokker E.I armed with a synchronized machine gun.

"but must seek them out and hunt them down." Immelmann predicted: "Things are going to be different."

They soon were. In July a Fokker E.I flown by Lieutenant Kurt Wintgens shot down an unsuspecting French Morane—although the kill could not be confirmed because the victim fell behind the Allied lines. Then, at 4:45 a.m. on the foggy morning of August 1, Immelmann reported, he "was awakened by a terrible row. About 10 enemy machines were cruising over our aerodrome at 8,000 to 10,000 feet and dropping bombs." The next thing Immelmann saw was Boelcke, still in his nightshirt, whizzing past on a motorbike to his E.I. Immelmann followed in the other Fokker.

By the time he reached altitude, Immelmann recounted, "I saw two opponents and Boelcke. I heard the rattle of machine guns. Suddenly I saw Boelcke go down in a steep dive." Boelcke's gun had jammed and he had to land to get it unstuck. Immelmann attacked alone.

"I dived on him like a hawk and fired my machine gun," he wrote. "For a moment I thought I was going to fly right into him." The other plane tried to turn away, but Immelmann "flew alongside him and cut off his line of retreat." Immelmann climbed again, attacked, then repeated the maneuver. At last the other plane went down in a steep glide, with the E.I on its tail. "When I saw him land," Immelmann wrote, "I went down beside him, climbed out, and went up to him." The downed pilot held out his right hand. "I shook hands and said: 'Bonjour, monsieur,' but he answered in English.

" 'Ah, you are an Englishman?'

" 'Yes.'

" 'You are my prisoner.'

" 'My arm is broken; you shot very well.' "

Boelcke's turn came 19 days later; firing through the propeller of his new Fokker, he shot down a British biplane. Before the month was out a number of brand-new Fokkers, just arrived from Schwerin, attacked a flight of nine French bombers and sent them all crashing to earth. The tide definitely had turned. On the last day of August, France lost Adolphe Pégoud. Wounded in the air by German bullets, he managed to land, but he died before he could be pulled from the cockpit. At his death he was the leading pilot in the world with six victories. For this he received the Légion d'Honneur and a hero's funeral. A solemn cortege of his grieving comrades followed his casket to the cemetery at Belfort, where he had fallen. Germans paid their respects too, flying unhindered over his gravesite to drop a wreath covered with ribbons and bearing the inscription: "His adversary honors the Aviator Pégoud, fallen in combat for his fatherland."

Pégoud's funeral was symbolic of the dramatic change that Max Immelmann had predicted. Now it was the Allies' turn to complain of German superiority in firepower. British fliers spoke darkly of a "Fokker scourge," and of themselves as "Fokker fodder," even though only 15 or so of the E-series Fokkers were being delivered to their adversaries

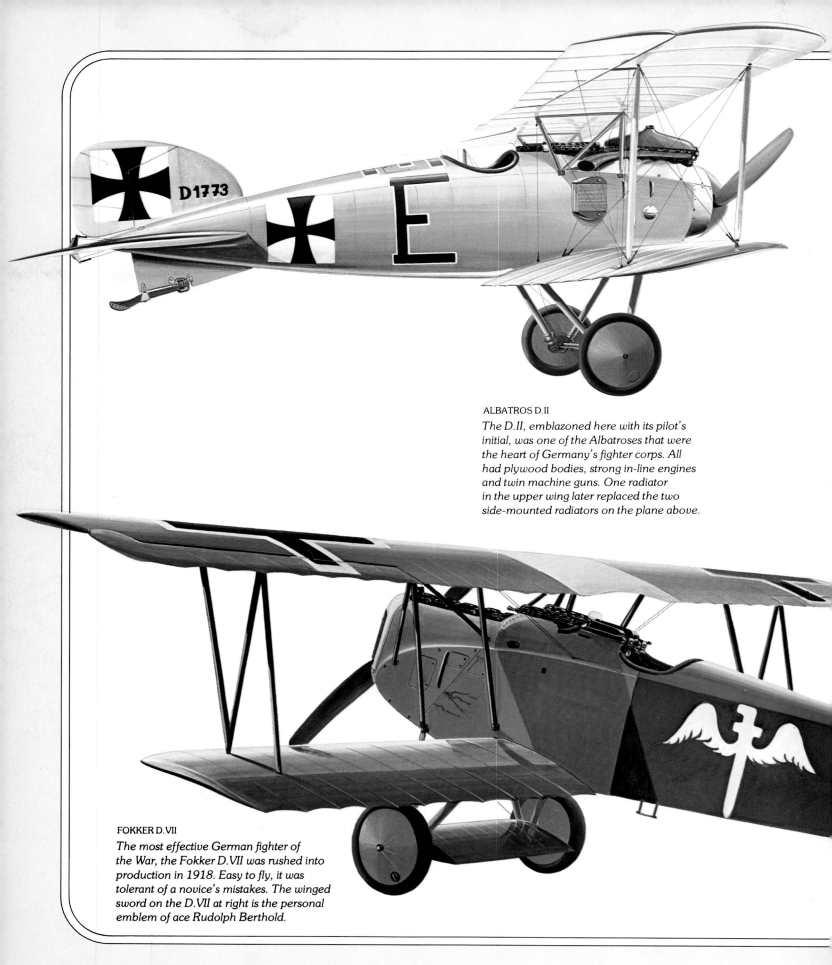

ALBATROS D.II

The D.II, emblazoned here with its pilot's initial, was one of the Albatroses that were the heart of Germany's fighter corps. All had plywood bodies, strong in-line engines and twin machine guns. One radiator in the upper wing later replaced the two side-mounted radiators on the plane above.

FOKKER D.VII

The most effective German fighter of the War, the Fokker D.VII was rushed into production in 1918. Easy to fly, it was tolerant of a novice's mistakes. The winged sword on the D.VII at right is the personal emblem of ace Rudolph Berthold.

Formidable fighters of the Central Powers

Outnumbered, the air forces of the Central Powers fought for years on nearly equal terms with the Allies owing in large part to the outstanding capabilities of their best fighter planes. In late summer of 1916 the Albatros D.I reached the front, followed within a few months by its successor, the D.II, seen at left (planes designated *D* were single-engined fighter biplanes). In the hands of pilots like Oswald Boelcke and Manfred von Richthofen, the streamlined Albatros was probably the best fighter of its day, a rapid climber with twice the firepower of contemporary Allied planes. The D.II and the even faster-climbing D.III that followed helped Germany to dominate the air over the Western Front through the spring of 1917.

Austria-Hungary equipped its air force with a German-designed biplane, the hardy Hansa-Brandenburg D.I *(be-low)*. Although obsolescent by the time it reached the Italian front in the fall of 1916, the plane nevertheless served as the Empire's work-horse fighter for almost a year.

Germany's best-known fighters were Fokkers. Early Fokker monoplanes, equipped with synchronized machine guns, for a time were the scourge of the Western Front, and later, the Fokker triplane *(pages 120-121)* served Richthofen's Flying Circus well. Most respected of all was the Fokker D.VII *(below, left)*, a biplane introduced in April of 1918. The D.VII could climb faster than the best Allied planes and was exceptionally maneuverable—and deadly—at high altitudes. The Allies held the D.VII in such esteem that, when the War ended, it was the only airplane specifically mentioned in the Armistice list of war matériel to be surrendered by the Germans.

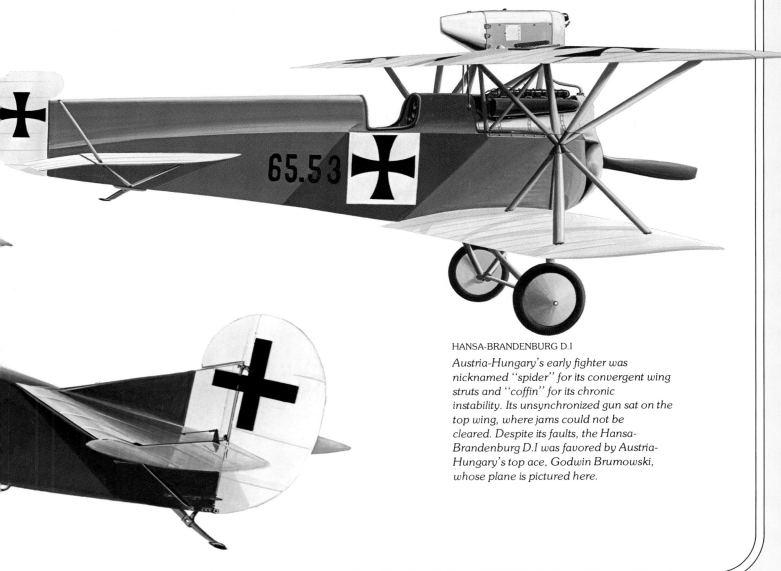

HANSA-BRANDENBURG D.I

Austria-Hungary's early fighter was nicknamed "spider" for its convergent wing struts and "coffin" for its chronic instability. Its unsynchronized gun sat on the top wing, where jams could not be cleared. Despite its faults, the Hansa-Brandenburg D.I was favored by Austria-Hungary's top ace, Godwin Brumowski, whose plane is pictured here.

each month. Just as the Germans had once responded to Allied superiority by racing for home, Allied pilots now learned to flee at the sight of the fearsome new German planes. "They treat my single-seater with a holy respect," said Boelcke. "They bolt as quick as they can." And Immelmann boasted, "There are no enemy machines in the air 10 minutes after Boelcke and I have appeared."

The Germans kept up the pressure. "I always go off to the lines in the evening with Lieutenant Immelmann to hunt the French," wrote Boelcke in mid-September. These outings netted the hunter-killers two more victories apiece through September and another pair each in October. A friendly rivalry, fueled by the German press, rose between them as the numbers mounted. Boelcke sneered at fancy flying in combat, regarding aerobatics as a last resort to be used only when he was up against a skillful foe who refused to hold still for a good shot. "When a fellow is in such a funk and is going into turns," Boelcke explained, "he can never hit anything. I on the other hand always wait for the favorable moment and put in a few well-directed shots."

In this Immelmann needed no persuasion. "I do not employ tricks when I attack," he said. Indeed, nowhere in his letters or other writings did Immelmann mention using the maneuver with which his name is connected to this day: the Immelmann turn, a half loop with a half roll on top. One British source suggests the maneuver was not Immelmann's at all, but got its name from an Allied pilot who used it to escape from a tail-end attack by the feared German.

Flying straight and often, the Fokker pilots achieved local dominance of the skies, though they were still outnumbered. During heavy ground attacks in September at Lens, and again at Arras, they cleared the air for the German reconnaissance planes, a new generation of armed two-seaters introduced by Albatros, Rumpler and other firms. These so-called C-class planes, with the observer seated behind the pilot for a better view, brought back trench-line photographs and other information that contributed to another terrible round of Allied casualties. With each new air victory Immelmann and Boelcke reaped greater honors. Chief of the General Staff Erich von Falkenhayn awarded Boelcke the Knight's Cross of the House of Hohenzollern with Swords, and Lieutenant Colonel von der Lieth-Thomsen told him, "All comrades of the air service look up to you with pride."

Boelcke indeed was the stuff of legends. Once, while in a German-occupied part of France, he jumped fully clad into a canal to haul out a boy who was drowning. The boy's grateful French parents wanted him to be awarded the Légion d'Honneur, a twist that Boelcke thought "would be a great joke."

Immelmann had also earned the respect of his foes. Britons nick-named him the Eagle of Lille, after the town in northern France above which he frequently prowled. Immelmann could not resist a certain amount of crowing over his celebrity. "It is incredible how much I am honored," he wrote home. "I get letters every day addressed: 'Flying

Advertising the wares of war

Although there were four Central Powers, Germany faced the challenge of matching the wartime industrial output of the Allies almost alone. German aircraft manufacturers responded with a patriotic urgency that is evident in the martial tone of their advertisements.

The company most often identified with the rise of German air power was owned by the transplanted Dutchman Anthony Fokker and headquartered at Schwerin in northern Germany. Early in the War, Fokker monoplanes, with machine guns adapted to fire between the blades of their spinning propellers, produced so many aces that by the autumn of 1916 nine Fokker pilots had been awarded the Pour le Mérite and the firm proudly displayed the cherished medal in its advertisements *(right)*.

But Fokker planes never made up more than a small part of the German air arsenal. The War Ministry fostered competition by awarding contracts to dozens of large and small firms for improved designs and faster production. The aircraft industry, barely more than a scattered collection of workshops on the eve of war, reached a production peak of 1,600 planes a month in 1917—still little more than half of the Allied effort for that year.

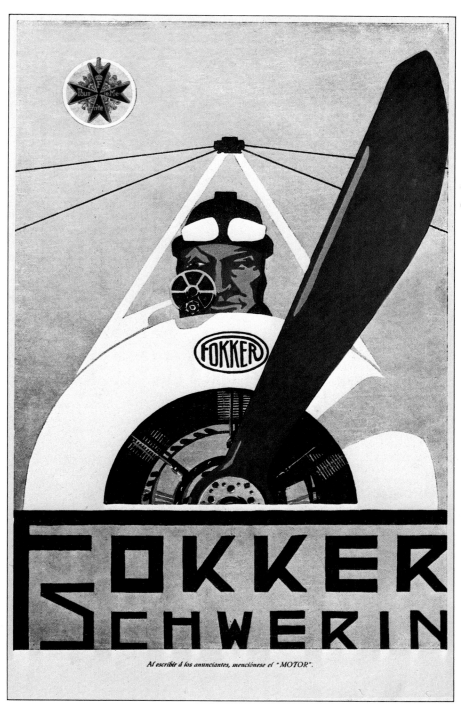

A pilot sights his machine gun past the propeller of his plane in this advertisement for the Fokker company, embellished with a Blue Max in the upper left corner.

Rumpler, originally known for its popular Taube monoplanes, built hundreds of reconnaissance biplanes during the War.

RUMPLER WERKE GM BH
BERLIN-JOHANNISTHAL
FLUGZEUGE
Militärfliegerschule · Müncheberg (Mark)

ALBATROS

GESELLSCHAFT FÜR FLUGZEUG-UNTER-
NEHMUNGEN M·B·H· BERLIN-JOHANNISTAL

Albatros was Germany's largest aircraft maker. At one time 60 per cent of German frontline fighters were Albatroses.

AVIATIK
Flugzeuge
AUTOMOBIL u. AVIATIK A.G. ✶ LEIPZIG ✶

Aviatik, which made automobiles as well as aircraft, moved to Leipzig in 1916, away from its location near the Western Front.

Oberursel rotary engines, at first made under license from a French firm, powered most Fokker fighter planes.

Luft-Verkehrs-Gesellschaft, or L.V.G., was founded in 1910; by 1918 the firm was producing 150 planes a month.

Garuda of Berlin made propellers for German aircraft, which the company grimly portrayed as agents of death.

Lieutenant Immelmann, Western Front,' and that is quite enough.''

There was little to crow about in the British sectors of the front. Though the RFC had received a number of improved single-seated front-engined planes—Bristols and Martinsydes—none had a synchronizer. In January 1916, RFC headquarters issued this rather desperate order: "Until the Royal Flying Corps are in possession of a machine as good or better than the German Fokker . . . it must be laid down as a hard and fast rule that a machine proceeding on reconnaissance must be escorted by at least three fighting machines."

One British airman sent home a vivid description of what it was like when a Fokker approached. "You feel naked and helpless. The panic seeps through your pores . . . everything seems unreal . . . and then you hear the guns hacking. All I can do at the controls is stay to a westerly course and summon every trick I know . . . swerving erratically from side to side so the Boche does not have a steady target. Only as a last shift do I give away altitude, since he can climb like an arrow off a bowstring and enjoys an absolute advantage if I go too low. . . . It is a harrowing, execrable ordeal."

In those grim times the Allies derived a measure of satisfaction from a bomber raid by 62 French planes on the German steel town of Dillingen and from follow-up strikes elsewhere in the Saar, where steel production temporarily dropped 30 per cent. But these triumphs were balanced by renewed dirigible raids on England that also did much to cut production. Twenty-two people were killed and 87 wounded in one attack on London and, on the day after a raid, absenteeism in factories ran as high as 20 per cent. The RFC was pressured into holding 110 potential frontline planes at home to calm civilian fears.

Whatever their morale problems, the Allies never lost their numerical superiority, and by concentrating their planes they could achieve temporary control of the air over a battlefield. But during the fall the British alone lost 26 planes in combat to the Germans' 11. One French aviator seemed to express the frustration of all when he deliberately flew into a Fokker's tail, his propeller chewing off the German's control surfaces. Both planes fell, but the Frenchman, as lucky as he was foolhardy, managed to glide his machine, with its shattered stub of a propeller, to a safe landing.

The German command spared the Allies the full brunt of its force by assigning the Fokkers by ones and twos to many sections instead of concentrating them in homogeneous fighting units. This error was compounded by a renewed order to fly only defensive missions, now called barrage patrols, over German lines. A number of the pilots ignored the order and attacked in enemy territory. By now they were flying an improved Fokker, the E.III, equipped with a 100-horsepower engine and sometimes two of the latest model machine guns, popularly called Spandaus after the Berlin suburb where they were produced. Each gun carried up to 600 rounds. Immelmann even persuaded Fokker to build him a special three-gun plane, in which he soon shot himself down—

without injury—when the synchronizing gears malfunctioned in the overburdened, nose-heavy aircraft.

In the first weeks of 1916, Germany began to concentrate its armies and a tremendous mass of artillery for a blow at Verdun, a heretofore impregnable bastion about 140 miles east of Paris. The build-up included 168 planes, 21 Fokkers among them. During the preparations, on January 12, Immelmann and Boelcke each scored his eighth victory. This time Kaiser Wilhelm himself took note, bestowing upon each of them Prussia's highest military honor, the blue-ribboned Pour le Mérite. Nicknamed the Blue Max, it had been given to German fighting men for almost two centuries but never before to a flier.

Each of the recipients reacted in his own way. Boelcke thought the news was a hoax; he believed it when he found himself fending off a general who "nearly killed himself with affability." On his way to a dinner in his honor with the King of Bavaria, he paused long enough to go up and knock down an Allied aircraft for his ninth kill. Immelmann was so excited he could not eat or drink anything that day. "I didn't know whether I was awake or dreaming," he wrote. Next evening, his appetite restored, he set off with comrades in an automobile to celebrate. The car ran over three chickens, which he cooked and washed down with champagne.

There was little time left for celebration. On February 21, fourteen hundred German guns let go in a 10-hour bombardment on an eight-mile front at Verdun. It was the start of a monstrous, year-long battle that Germany had to win and France could not afford to lose. ᜒᜒ

The impact of stress on master airman Oswald Boelcke of Germany is evident in these photographs, both taken in 1916. Below, he appears in a studio wearing at his collar the Blue Max he won in January; at right, lines of fatigue crease his face in October of the same year.

Making the most of life between missions

Aviators on both sides lived more comfortably than soldiers in the trenches. At best home might be a commandeered château where wine, cooks and batmen, and a range of sporting activities made for a highly civilized life.

To unwind, the airmen read, wrote letters, listened to music—and made their own *(below)*. Some squadrons became famous for boisterous parties; others organized variety shows. And, whenever possible, the airmen sought the night life of a city. "We existed," one Allied pilot remembered, "only for the times we could go to Paris."

Whatever the diversion, a flier had to be prepared to drop it at a moment's notice. Canada's Billy Bishop recalled a day he and other pilots were playing tennis when a sortie was ordered. "We were still in our white flannels," he wrote. "There was no time to change, so into the machines we crawled and started aloft."

A French pilot supplements the gramophone (foreground) with violin music for an attentive comrade at a barracks in 1916.

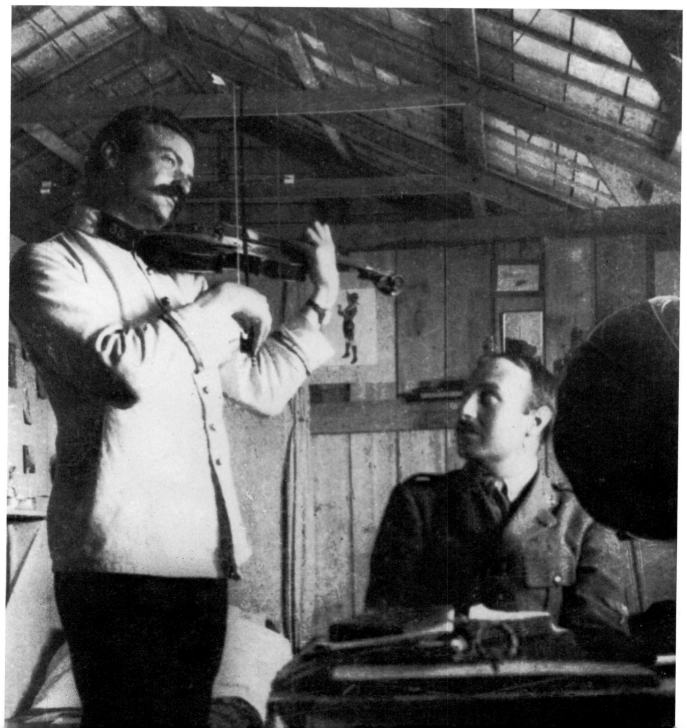

Aviators of Germany's Jasta 5—several in costume for the occasion—celebrate New Year's Eve 1917.

Attended by batmen, British flight officers serving in Italy in 1917 await their evening meal at a neatly set table.

French ace Gabriel Thomas reads about French aces.

A British airman takes careful aim during a game of billards.

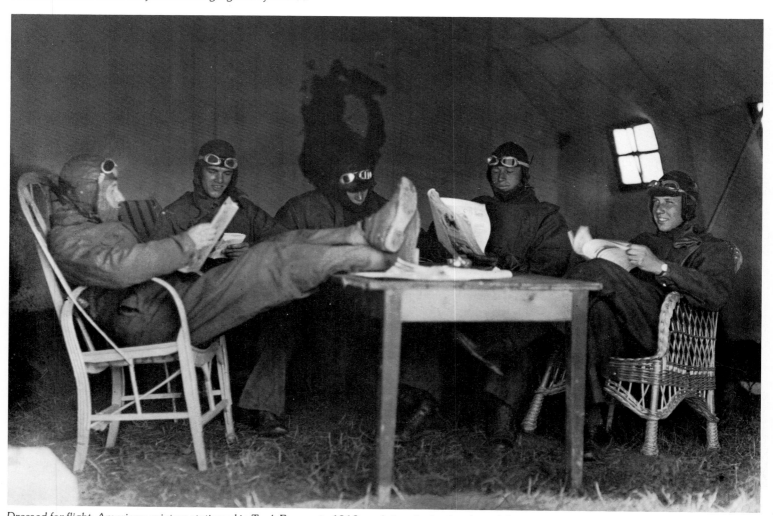

Dressed for flight, American aviators stationed in Toul, France, in 1918 mark time in the duty hut while awaiting the signal to take off.

A vaudeville troupe, organized from the American 20th Aero Squadron, traveled to its performances in a well-marked truck.

German fliers relax at cards in a commandeered château. The tapestry at rear has been defaced by having airplanes drawn on it.

3
The Allies ascendant

The specter of the Fokker scourge continued to haunt the Western Front during the great winter offensive of 1916 as the German Army, determined to "bleed France white," hammered relentlessly at Verdun. Each side had assembled more than 500 planes along the front, most of them concentrated around the fortified French town. For months, however, the Germans had been knocking down several times as many French and British planes as they lost themselves. Morale, and performance, in the Allied air services sorely needed a lift.

The lift came, thanks in large measure to the drive and vision of two officers who staked the future of the air war on a simple but controversial premise: "Carry the war into enemy territory and keep it there." The words were those of General Hugh Montague Trenchard, commander of the Royal Flying Corps in France, who was known throughout the ranks as Boom, both for the timbre of his voice and for the impact generated by his pronouncements. His philosophy was summed up in the words "strategic offensive," which he described as "leaning forward over German territory constantly."

Early in 1916, Trenchard ordered his fighter planes to "raid prominent enemy aerodromes and attack any hostile machine that offers combat." He knew the cost would be high: Green pilots and obsolescent aircraft would too often be sent to obliteration far from the safety of their own lines. But he gambled that this calculated recklessness would undermine Germany's capacity to fight in the air, while it would revive the spirit of his own aviators. However, Lanoe Hawker, now commander of No. 24 Squadron, wrote his family: "I'm strictly forbidden to cross the lines, squadron commanders being (I suppose) too valuable."

Trenchard found a disciple and collaborator in Jean Du Peuty, a major who was commandant of a French air unit at beleaguered Verdun. Du Peuty had to fight off not only the Fokkers but the influence of French army commanders, who wanted French air strength used entirely for close support. Gradually he was able to organize his fighters into independent groups "outside the ordinary army cooperation squadrons," thus, as he wrote Trenchard in April, "freeing the real combat aircraft for independent offensive action."

Trenchard had ordered his pilots to practice the protective discipline of formation flying. Du Peuty went a step further, instructing his men to fly in "an echeloned formation in three dimensions," with the aircraft

Italian bombers wreak destruction and terror in this contemporary illustration of a raid on the Austrian airdrome at Prosecco in 1916, a year when offense became accepted as the key to air tactics.

aligned in steps above and behind the formation leader—an arrangement that became a permanent part of air tactics.

Four of France's best escadrilles at Verdun were organized into a special fighter group under Major Tricornot de Rose that became known as *Les Cigognes*—"The Storks." Each escadrille flew into battle with a different version of the stork, the heraldic symbol of German-held Alsace and a popular omen of good luck, painted on its fuselages. The Storks' orders were concise: "Seek the enemy in order to engage and destroy him." Few orders in military history have been carried out with such panache, as the pride of French aviation—often ignoring Du Peuty's dictum to stay in formation—fought to regain control of the sky.

In the air, as on the ground, the fortunes of battle fluctuated almost daily. The German fighters tended their reconnaissance planes like sheep dogs protecting a flock. On those occasions when they broke away for offensive action, the Germans still were capable of turning the air over Verdun into what Oswald Boelcke called his "shooting pond." His victory total rose to a dozen and more. But too often the defensive mentality prevailed and as a result the Germans failed to press home their midwinter advantage. In one two-week period the French Army reinforced Verdun with 190,000 men and 22,500 tons of munitions, keeping 8,000 trucks moving day and night along a single 36-mile road. The German planes that might have shut down the road never appeared, and heartened French soldiers began calling it *la Voie Sacrée*—"the Sacred Way."

In March, Boelcke reported to his superiors that "The French are flying more keenly now and in larger crowds." Indeed, as Trenchard and Du Peuty had intended, thicker and more disciplined flights of Allied planes had begun each day to break through the German barrage patrols and cross the lines. One such flight fought off attacks by 14 German aircraft and returned to base without losing a plane.

In response the German command moved some of its airdromes closer to the front, the better to challenge intruding British and French planes, and they set up three new all-fighter groups and allotted six to nine Fokkers to each of them. But by now the Fokkers were coming up against Allied planes that could match or surpass them. During the winter the Royal Flying Corps received two new models that were the latest and best of the British pusher designs: the two-seated F.E.2b and the D.H.2, a single-seated plane with a front-mounted machine gun. France had developed a big brother to its Nieuport *Bébé,* the Nieuport 17, with a 110-horsepower Le Rhône engine that, as one delighted pilot said, "could climb like a witch," reaching an altitude of 10,000 feet in just over 10 minutes.

Germany's monopoly on the synchronized machine gun also was about to end. With a belated sense of urgency, the British and the French that winter had independently developed several different synchronizing systems. On March 25 the first Allied synchronizer reached the front, fitted to an otherwise obsolescent Bristol Scout; within several months a majority of Allied fighter planes would have them. Meanwhile, the reputation of the Fokker as a weapon of almost mystical superiority suffered a severe deflation in an incident in which the new Allied synchronizer played no part.

On April 8 an inexperienced German pilot lost his way while ferrying a new Fokker to the front and landed at an Allied airfield by mistake. His plane was captured intact, and it was decided to test it, head to head, against a comparable Allied aircraft. The plane chosen was the latest Morane-Saulnier monoplane, nicknamed the Bullet.

The two planes took off together and, to the astonishment of most of those watching, the Morane-Saulnier immediately demonstrated its superiority. It climbed more quickly, went faster in level flight and, in mock combat, had a clear edge over the much-feared German fighter. "A cheer went up from the ground," reported one exuberant eyewitness. "The bogey was laid."

As Trenchard had predicted, Allied morale stiffened as the offensive tactics, buttressed by improved aircraft, brought an end to Fokker domination. As Allied spirits rose, German confidence faded. In April Lanoe Hawker reported that when Allied planes crossed the lines, a few Fokkers would come up and "hang like minnows in a stream, but they would not fight." And by late May Lieutenant General Henry Rawlinson of the British Fourth Army could report flatly, "We have command of the air."

The seemingly endless battle in the forts and trenches of Verdun was far from decided, however; it would last almost to the year's end and the combined French and German casualties would mount to some three quarters of a million dead, wounded and missing. In June the French, anxious to divert public attention from the carnage on the ground, decided to single out for attention those aviators who had scored at least five confirmed victories in the air. Soon a pilot who met this standard was publicly dubbed an ace; his victory count was published in a running box score in the French press and often he became the focus of a barrage of patriotically inspired publicity. Much of this attention went to the Storks and to an escadrille of American volunteers who had persuaded the authorities to let them fly for France as a unit, even though their nation was still at peace. Thus the world became aware of a handful of colorful individual champions and began avidly to follow their adventures, both in the air and on the ground.

Germany had already begun to pay homage to its air heroes: Postcards of Max Immelmann wearing his Blue Max flooded the land, and an operatic aria was rewritten as a tribute to Boelcke. The Germans eventually adopted the French ace system, but with 10 victories as a minimum requirement. They called a flier who reached that plateau *kanone*, or "top gun." The British never officially recognized the designation ace; Boom Trenchard, for one, thought it brought undue acclaim to the fighter pilot and diminished the valiant, often sacrificial efforts of

Major General Hugh M. Trenchard, the commander of the Royal Flying Corps in France, scorned use of the airplane for defense and favored "relentless and incessant" offensive action instead. "The sky," he wrote, "is too large to defend."

the observers and gunners. But Britain needed heroes too, and British heroes soon emerged from the caldron of Trenchard's offensive action over eastern France.

The most flamboyant, and tireless, of the newly fledged Allied aces was a 20-year-old French sublieutenant, Jean Navarre. Navarre spent as many as nine or 10 hours a day in the air over Verdun, coming down only to refuel his plane, reload his guns and revive his energies with light food and wine. Flying Nieuports in a combination of headlong attacks and masterful aerobatics, he shot down 10 German planes in less than three months; by the end of May his total of 12 official kills led the scores of all Allied pilots.

Not far behind Navarre, with seven victories, was blond, athletic Charles Nungesser. As a teenager Nungesser had gone on his own to South America, where he had learned to fight with his fists, to drive racing cars—and to fly. He returned home to France to volunteer when war seemed imminent.

More than any other aviators, Nungesser and Navarre were responsible for creating the image of World War I aces as handsome, hard-living rakes without a care for tomorrow. Both of them chafed under military discipline; they particularly despised formation flying, which they regarded as constricting nonsense. Off duty they traveled to Paris as often as the demands of war allowed and pursued a good time with the same vigor they displayed while chasing German planes.

Navarre dressed for combat in unmistakable style: shaggy bearskin coat, leather breeches, fur-lined boots and gloves—and the silk stocking of a lady friend wrapped around his head. Nungesser was even less conventional. He occasionally reported for a dawn mission still dressed in a tuxedo or cutaway and accompanied by a woman. He often had to be helped into the cockpit, not usually from lack of sobriety but because he had been injured so often in air battles and in automobile accidents while driving at breakneck speed between the airfield and the night spots of Paris. One of the automobiles in which he did this whirlwind commuting was an elegant German staff car that he and two comrades had captured, after killing its occupants, during the 1914 retreat toward the Marne. But his favorite vehicle was a handsome yellow touring car he had bought from Adolphe Pégoud before Pégoud crashed to his death in 1915.

One evening, as Nungesser was impatiently negotiating the clogged road to Paris in the yellow car, a fine cigar as usual clamped between his remaining teeth, he noticed a distinctly familiar airplane passing overhead in the same direction. It turned out to be Nungesser's own plane, piloted by Navarre; they met at the edge of the city and Navarre explained unabashedly that his own plane had been shot up and that he had been so busy fighting the War he no longer remembered what a woman was like; he had come to Paris for a refresher. Together, the two aces set off for a boisterous night on the town.

Nungesser could scarcely complain because Navarre had borrowed

A pantheon of French aces

More, probably, than any other nation, France lionized its airmen. Even before the War, flamboyant stunt pilots like Adolphe Pégoud *(below)* were national heroes, and once the fighting began, these experienced French fliers earned still greater renown as they pioneered techniques of aerial combat. Pégoud was the first to achieve the five victories that became the requirement for the coveted title "ace."

The term itself was coined in France and developed into a semiofficial ranking system for fighter pilots. Military communiqués citing the aces' exploits were regularly released to the press, and many of the fliers singled out were then assigned to the highly publicized Stork escadrilles.

Public adulation seemed to encourage the French aces in their already marked individuality. Many of them scorned formation flying and other team aspects of air combat, each preferring to confront the enemy in his own way. René Fonck, who became France's top-ranking ace, favored solo missions so that he could, as he put it, "perform those little coups of audacity which amused me." Charles Nungesser, celebrated for his reckless bravery, once charged knowingly into an aerial ambush in response to a personal challenge dropped from a German plane. Even Georges Guynemer, dutiful and reticent on the ground, went his own zealous way in the air.

The loss of a prominent flier was a national calamity. When Guynemer disappeared over Belgium in September 1917, the War Ministry hesitated to declare him missing—and the public refused to accept the news when it came. On the following pages appear France's eight highest-scoring aces, five of whom survived the War.

ADOLPHE PÉGOUD had six victories, more than any other flier in the War, when he was shot down in August 1915.

CHARLES NUNGESSER (45 victories) disappeared
in 1927 while trying to fly the Atlantic.

GEORGES GUYNEMER (54 victories) was second
among French aces but first in his nation's heart.

LÉON BOURJADE (28 victories), a seminarian,
became a leading balloon buster and later a missionary.

GEORGES MADON (41 victories) once safely
landed his plane after a shell blew the engine away.

ARMAND PINSARD (27 victories) received France's
first air citation for bombing a German headquarters.

MAURICE BOYAU (35 victories), France's national
rugby captain, was shot down attacking a balloon.

RENÉ FONCK (75 victories) went on to become a
celebrated postwar exhibition pilot.

MICHEL COIFFARD (34 victories) downed 28
German balloons before he died in October 1918.

his plane; it was a similar practice that had made him a fighter pilot to begin with. Early in his career he had been assigned to reconnaissance duty. One day he borrowed a brand new Voisin he had been admiring and, taking his gunner with him, went up before dawn determined to get his first victory. No sooner was he aloft than five German planes were reported approaching the airdrome. The squadron commander sent out a call for the duty pilot—who happened to be Nungesser—and ordered up the new Voisin. Of course neither could be found. As the commander fumed, the phone rang with word that someone had just shot down one of the Germans. Nungesser landed to receive a commendation for the Croix de Guerre and eight days' arrest. He was soon assigned to fighter training, where his talents might be better used.

Delighted at the sight of his first Nieuport, Nungesser painted on it the insignia that would become his trademark: a large skull and crossbones set below a coffin adorned by a candle at either end. It was a flouting of death that fitted his style. Not long after, he crashed-landed, breaking both his legs, dislocating his jaw and perforating his palate. A less healthy man might have been killed, and even Nungesser could never again walk properly without a cane. As soon as he had partially healed, he announced he was going back "to relax at the front." Rejoining his escadrille at Verdun, he knocked down four German planes and a balloon in quick succession. The last plane was flying at the rear of a formation of six; the others turned on Nungesser but he maneuvered into the midst of them with such skill that the Germans had to hold fire for fear of hitting one another, and he escaped.

The uniforms of both Nungesser and Navarre fairly clanked with decorations; Nungesser was so proud of his medals that he wore them everywhere, even into combat. But both men seemed driven toward disaster. On June 17, Jean Navarre went down over the Argonne Forest, so badly shot up he never again flew in combat. Nungesser was also wounded again in June and was out of action for a month.

To replace this freewheeling pair, France produced a young flier of dramatically different stripe, one who could be counted on to obey orders, to behave impeccably and to fly with precision—and, of course, with a large measure of dash. Georges Guynemer seemed inspired, and, in turn, he inspired others. Before long the boy who in 1914 had dreamed of flight on the beach at Biarritz would be lionized as "the Winged Sword of France . . . the purest symbol of France's national ideals." Guynemer said the kind of things knights are supposed to say: "I owe myself to my country," "Never talk to me about going to the rear" and "Death is the risk of the profession, but far rather that than captivity."

Such words came naturally from this scion of a family as old as France itself. An ancient heroic poem lauded a Guynemer of the Eighth Century who rode with Charlemagne against Spain. Another ancestor, while still a boy at the time of the French Revolution, faced down the fearsome Robespierre to save his condemned schoolmistress, so that he

Dashing Jean Navarre stands in the cockpit of a Morane monoplane equipped with deflectors to protect its propeller from the unsynchronized fire of its machine gun. Once, in the days before planes were equipped with fixed guns, Navarre took off after a Zeppelin armed with a kitchen knife. Despite his recklessness, he survived the War only to die practicing a stunt for a 1919 victory parade.

might resume his lessons. Georges's rush to enlist at the outbreak of war demonstrated that he was cut from the same cloth as his ancestors.

Guynemer learned to fly at Pau early in 1915 in an old three-cylinder Blériot, and from the start his zeal was unquenchable if somewhat unsettling. His instructor's report chided him for "too much confidence, madness, fantastical humor." In June he arrived at the front near Vauciennes as a corporal-pilot in Escadrille M.S.3 under Captain Felix Brocard. That battle-toughened officer gave Guynemer the impression that "I was a boy who amused him." Small wonder. After one patrol Guynemer's officer-observer reported that at the end of an hour's reconnaissance under heavy fire, the young pilot had insisted upon flying straight at the enemy guns. Handing the officer his personal camera, Guynemer asked him to take some pictures of the projectiles as they exploded around the plane. Back at the field, his excitement unabated, he proudly showed Brocard the plane's shrapnel holes, and insisted that he probe them with his fingers.

Guynemer's first victory, a month later, merely whetted his enthusiasm. His account of the clash, with an Aviatik above Soissons, reveals a single-minded eagerness only partly explained by his youth. "Everybody in the city watched the fantastic duel over their heads," he told a journalist later. "I kept about 15 meters from my Boche and, notwithstanding all his twistings, I managed not to lose touch with him." Guynemer's gunner fired 115 shots and was grazed twice himself. Then, Guynemer reported, "I had a very sweet feeling at seeing the pilot slump to the floor of his cockpit, while the lookout raised his arms to heaven in a gesture of despair and the Aviatik plunged down into the abyss in flames." The vanquished plane fell between the trenches. "I hastened to land nearby," said Guynemer, "and I can guarantee that I never felt a greater elation than at that moment." So great was Guynemer's haste, in fact, that he ran the nose of his two-seater into a haystack and broke the propeller.

Despite his boyishness, Guynemer's spirit and audacity began to earn his commandant's admiration. He was showing himself to be a fearless war lover who knew how to put his plane right next to an enemy's when the shooting started. Recommended for fighter training in Nieuports, Guynemer celebrated by stunting his plane over his family's house at nearby Compiègne. After landing he excitedly wrote home: "Did you see me?" "Yes," responded his father, "and the performance scared your mother half to death." Guynemer replied contritely that he felt "wretched to know that my veering frightened Mama."

On a Sunday morning in December 1915, he scored a second victory, his first in a Nieuport *Bébé*, hurling himself at a German plane that proceeded to fall into a tailspin not far from Compiègne. But Guynemer lost sight of the place where the enemy airplane had fallen. Again he landed in a field near his home, waited for his family to return from Mass, then rushed up to them.

"Father," he said, "I have lost my Boche. Look for him and find him." Leaving his somewhat bewildered parent to locate the wreck of the German aircraft and thus confirm the kill, Guynemer took off again, gunning his engine as he approached the airdrome to announce his latest triumph.

By Christmas Eve, the day he turned 21, he had four victories, had been promoted to sergeant and had received the Légion d'Honneur as a "pilot of great value, model of devotion and courage." Though he would never lose his passion to fly and fight, he was beginning to mature. His mechanic's training had blossomed into a sure knowledge of the Nieuport's engine and structure, and his gunnery had grown deadly through practice. Before taking off, he would walk silently around his Nieuport for several minutes, examining each screw and bolt and wire stay, running his fingertips over the covering fabric to find flaws, checking the alignment of his Lewis gun. As he removed his kepi and pulled on his flying suit, he grew tense with concentration. At that moment, said a comrade, "his eyes were like blows."

Guynemer's flying style matured along with his demeanor. Except as a "last means," he never took "recourse to aerobatics." Instead, he explained, "my method consists in attacking almost point blank. It is more risky, but everything lies in maneuvering so as to remain in the dead angle of fire."

Proving the latter point soon almost cost him his life. In March of 1916 his escadrille was ordered to Verdun. Guynemer, now a second lieutenant, could hardly wait. "I considered it a feast to be able to take part in the great battle," he said, and on the way to his new station he overtook and attacked a German plane. "A few shots, fire! It was all over," he reported. It was his eighth victory.

But Verdun, where the best of the German air force had gathered, was a different matter. On his first day there, Guynemer took on two Germans, sent one of them scampering "with lead in his wings," then snapped around to attack the other from below. "He was certainly an ace," Guynemer said later in some chagrin. "He was not afraid and fired as hard as he could." Evidently Guynemer went in too impulsively, for he suddenly found himself ahead of his opponent and taking a "hot fire" of machine-gun bullets. Two bullets thudded into his left arm. Another slashed his cheek and nose. Half blinded by blood, he plunged 1,000 feet, straightened out just above the ground and, "steering with one hand," managed to escape, his airplane all but demolished.

For three months the wounds kept a frustrated Guynemer grounded, but he returned in June—just in time to take up the slack left by the disabling of Nungesser and Navarre. The Allies were about to launch a massive assault across the River Somme in the hope of pulling the weight of German arms away from Verdun. On the ground it would be preponderantly a British show. Originally, France had planned to put 40 divisions into the Somme attack, but many of the men lay dead at Verdun. Instead France sent 16 divisions and 201 planes—including six escadrilles of Nieuports under Captain Brocard.

Movable bases on an immobile front

Western Europe was dotted from Switzerland to the North Sea with the airdromes of Germany and the Allies. Both sides built scores of new airfields to supplement those that were already established before the War. The map at right shows 61 of them.

Some of the airdromes were permanent military installations. But the majority, sometimes no farther than 7 miles from the front lines, were little more than collections of quickly constructed huts, tents and hangars huddled near open fields. At some airdromes herds of cattle grazed undisturbed among the planes. Few airfields were in constant use. When fighting flared nearby, an airfield would become the hub of intense activity for weeks or months at a time; then, as local combat subsided, the field would be relegated to a secondary role—or abandoned altogether.

The Western Front itself shifted very little from late 1914 until the closing weeks of the War. Lines on the map show the greatest variations: The broken line indicates the extent of Germany's deepest penetration into Belgium and France in September 1914; the solid line marks the limits of the Allies' final push in 1918, which ended on November 11 with the Armistice.

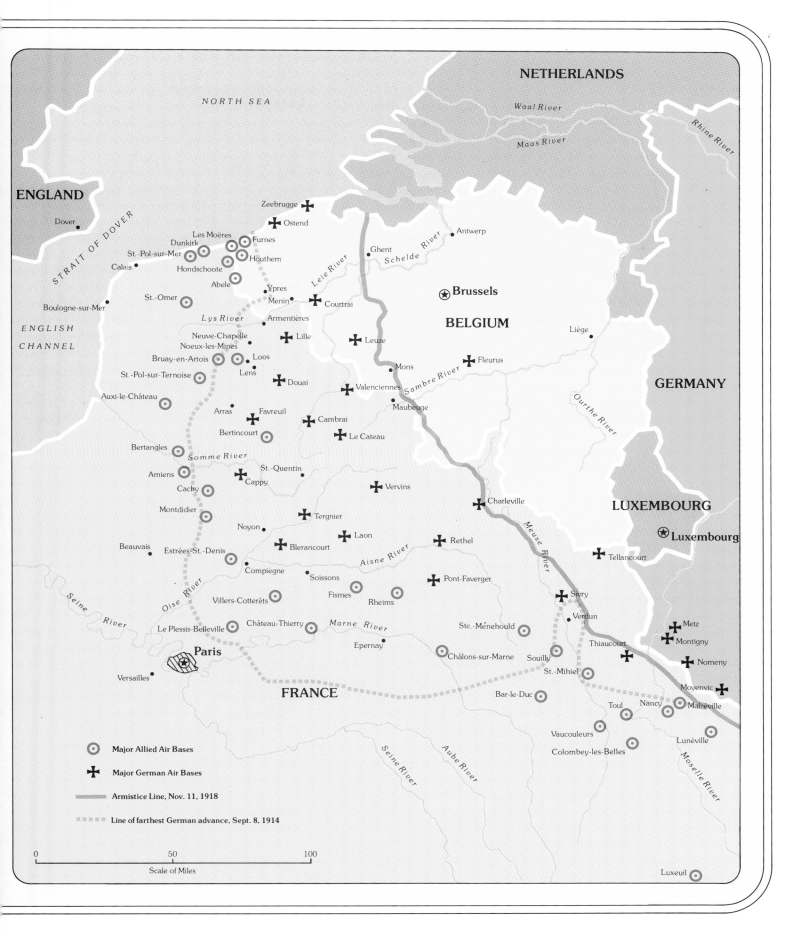

NETHERLANDS

NORTH SEA

Waal River

Maas River

Rhine River

ENGLAND

Dover

STRAIT OF DOVER

Zeebrugge ✠

✠ Ostend

Les Moëres
Dunkirk
Furnes ◉
St.-Pol-sur-Mer ◉ ◉ ◉
Calais
Hondschoote
Houthem
Abele
St.-Omer ◉
Boulogne-sur-Mer

ENGLISH CHANNEL

Ghent
Antwerp

Schelde River

Leie River

★ Brussels

BELGIUM

Liége

Ypres
Menin
✠ Courtrai
Lys River
Armentières
Neuve-Chapelle ✠ Lille
Noeux-les-Mines
Bruay-en-Artois ◉ ◉ Loos
St.-Pol-sur-Ternoise ◉ Lens
Auxi-le-Château ◉
✠ Douai
✠ Leuze
✠ Fleurus
Mons
✠ Valenciennes
Maubeuge

Sambre River

GERMANY

Ourthe River

Arras ✠ Favreuil
Bertincourt ◉
✠ Cambrai
✠ Le Cateau

Bertangles ◉
Somme River
Amiens ◉
Cachy ◉
St.-Quentin
✠ Cappy

Montdidier ◉
✠ Vervins
✠ Charleville

LUXEMBOURG

★ Luxembourg

Beauvais
Estrées-St.-Denis ◉
Noyon
✠ Tergnier
✠ Laon
✠ Blerancourt
✠ Rethel
Aisne River
Meuse River
✠ Tellancourt

Oise River
Compiègne
Soissons
Villers-Cotterêts ◉
Fismes ◉
Rheims ◉
✠ Pont-Faverger
✠ Sivry
Verdun
✠ Metz
✠ Montigny

Seine River
Le Plessis-Belleville ◉
Château-Thierry ◉
Marne River
Epernay
Ste.-Ménehould ◉
Thiaucourt
✠ Nomeny

Paris
Versailles
Châlons-sur-Marne
Souilly
St.-Mihiel ◉
Moyenvic ✠

FRANCE
Bar-le-Duc ◉
Toul
Nancy ◉ Malzéville
Vaucouleurs ◉
Lunéville ◉
Colombey-les-Belles
Moselle River

Seine River
Aube River

◉ Major Allied Air Bases

✠ Major German Air Bases

▬▬ Armistice Line, Nov. 11, 1918

▪ ▪ ▪ Line of farthest German advance, Sept. 8, 1914

0   50   100
Scale of Miles

Luxeuil ◉

Britain had 185 aircraft to put into service over the Somme, with virtually all the fighter planes concentrated into specialized squadrons. Lanoe Hawker's No. 24 Squadron was enlarged from 12 to 18 D.H.2s and sent to join the French units at Cachy, where the Allied airmen began to fly joint missions.

When they were not flying, the aviators worked hard at forgetting the war around them. The British amused themselves by buzzing neighboring squadrons and bombing their friends with tennis balls. Such raids brought reprisals from ground parties armed with seltzer bottles and insect spray guns. Tipsy armistices celebrated the nightly cessation of mock hostilities. The typical climax for one of these roisterous affairs was a rugby scrum held either in the mess hut or in an empty hangar. Hawker himself, now a respected major of 25 but still one of the boys after hours, was knocked unconscious during one celebration.

Such horseplay reflected not only the extreme youthfulness of the fliers but also the rise in morale that Trenchard had hoped for now that the Allies had taken the offensive in the air. Preparing the way for the Somme attack, Guynemer, Hawker and their comrades roared over the lines in waves to blow trucks off the roads, shoot up locomotives and strafe the trenches, while reconnaissance planes photographed the entire German trench system facing the British Fourth Army.

On June 18 the German Air Service sustained a severe blow. Max Immelmann crashed to his death. The Eagle of Lille, whose victories totaled 15, had been given a command of his own less than a week before. The British claimed that he had fallen under attack by an F.E.2b, but the Germans disagreed. A comrade flying beside Immelmann said the ace actually had been attacking the F.E.2b but had shot himself down when his synchronizer gear malfunctioned. A study of the wreck, which fell on the German side, showed one propeller blade chopped off at precisely the line of Immelmann's gunfire.

Germany went into national mourning at the loss. Oswald Boelcke flew to Douai for a funeral that might have been staged for a Wagnerian opera: "Immelmann lay in state most wonderfully in the courtyard of a hospital," he wrote later. "All around him were obelisks, with torches on them. Various princes were present, including the Crown Princes of Bavaria and Saxony, and more than 20 generals."

Boelcke had lost his friendly rival for primacy among German aces. His own score stood at 18, more than that of any man on either side. On his return to his base he found orders to report at once to the chief of the Air Service. Boelcke, at 25, had recently become the youngest captain in the German Air Service. He assumed he would be ordered to the Somme, where the signs of an Allied build-up were unmistakable. Instead he was told he had been grounded until further notice. With Immelmann dead, Germany could not afford to lose its other air hero. He would report to a spa at Charleville for limited duty.

Boelcke exploded. Was he truly expected "to sit in a cold water sanatorium and take over the job of leading a crowd of weak-nerved

In a pilot's-eye view of the battered Somme battlefield, French infantrymen advance through smoke from an exploded German grenade depot.

French soldiers man the mooring lines of a partially inflated balloon being filled with hydrogen gas from cylinders on trucks.

Hazardous duty in airborne sausages

Captive balloons, anchored by steel cables to the ground, were less glamorous than planes, but their contribution to air observation was just as important. Used by both sides, the gas-filled "sausages" hovered near the lines to direct artillery fire and monitor enemy movements.

Each balloon was manned by an observer and his assistant, who telephoned reports to the ground. Barely maneuverable and unarmed, balloons were inviting targets. But they were resolutely defended by antiaircraft guns, and the balloonists usually wore parachutes.

German ground troops watch as a balloon begins its ascent on the Western Front.

Its basket a tiny speck, a British balloon hovers over the shell-smashed battlefield at Ypres. Balloons generally were tethered two to five miles inside friendly lines and reached heights up to 5,000 feet.

The simultaneous end of two German balloons, shot down near Boyelles, France, is recorded in a remarkable photograph. Attacking airplanes fired incendiary bullets to ignite the highly flammable gasbags, which would disintegrate in 20 seconds or less.

pilots in need of rest?'' Boelcke telephoned the Kaiser himself, who only reiterated the grounding order. Wilhelm did, however, approve a different assignment that would keep Boelcke out of danger: He was ordered to tour the Turkish and Russian fronts. Still far from happy, Boelcke stormed off to the airfield and shot down number 19. Then he packed and headed east, remarking glumly that his experience and ability might have been put to good use against the offensive that he was certain would soon begin.

British guns launched the Battle of the Somme at the end of June with a barrage so intense that it seemed impossible anything could survive it. For nine days the cannonading never stopped. British flier Cecil Lewis reported that the enemy lines were under a drifting cloud of high explosives. "Square miles of country were ripped and blasted to a pockmarked desolation. Trenches had been obliterated, flattened out."

Everything the Allies could put in the air had been sent over the Somme on rotating missions. On the afternoon of June 25, British planes assaulted 15 German observation balloons hovering over the front and brought down eight of them—some by means of rockets mounted on wing struts—without loss. Aircraft were assigned to skim low over the inferno, signaling to the ground with klaxon horns so that the artillery barrage could roll safely ahead of the advancing infantry. German aircraft were to be denied access to the battlefield by attacks on their airdromes.

Just after dawn on July 1, the bombardment crescendoed, and starting at 7:30 a.m., 66,000 tommies went over the top in waves along an 18-mile front. Local storm clouds and rain at first kept most aircraft on the ground, but when the klaxon planes did sweep over the battlefield, calling with raucous urgency, few soldiers answered. Most of them were dead or wounded—30,000 in the first hour. By day's end almost 60,000 casualties lay on the torn earth, chopped down by German machine gunners and cannoneers who had somehow survived by burrowing into their deeply dug shelters, not emerging until the attack began. Despite all preparations, aerial and otherwise, the British fell in larger numbers than had any assault force before them in history.

This day of disaster on the ground produced a series of Allied successes in the air. In early afternoon a strike by unmolested Allied bombers knocked out an ammunition train between Cambrai and Aubigny-au-Bac. Another attack at St. Quentin blew up 60 ammunition cars and damaged so much other matériel that an entire regiment had to return to the rear to reequip.

German bombers and fighter planes never touched a British soldier that day. Major L. W. B. Rees earned the Victoria Cross by single-handedly taking on a flight of about 10 German bombers and sending them packing for home.

How much more of a disaster the first days of the Somme would have been for the Allies without air superiority is difficult to imagine. Despite

THE LAST LOOP

The British used posters like these as training aids to alert inexperienced pilots to the pitfalls of aerial combat. The poster above shows the tail breaking off a victorious British plane—a warning against gratuitous aerobatics. The scene at right above emphasizes the danger of accepting an easy target at face value. The poster at bottom illustrates a favorite tactic: to attack from out of the blinding sun.

DECOYED

BEWARE OF THE HUN IN THE SUN

the grievous losses, the ground offensive pushed on; during that long summer of attack, pause and attack, the Allied air strikes never eased up. Over a four-month period French and British planes hit nearly 300 targets with 17,600 bombs. Clusters of observation balloons and swarms of reconnaissance planes directed Allied artillery fire with withering effect. In September, spotting planes attached to the British Fourth Army pinpointed 29 German guns that were then silenced by counter-battery fire. Allied strafing became so intimidating that in one action 370 German troops gave themselves up to a raiding party of Leicester infantry after waving white handkerchiefs in surrender to a machine-gunning British plane.

Swamped by superior numbers, German air units were almost no help to the embattled infantry and artillery. German airfields came under constant attack. "Enemy airplanes in squadrons of six, eight, 10 and more worked over our airdromes," related a German pilot. The life expectancy of a German frontline pilot fell to a new low; more than one replacement died only minutes after taking off on his first mission.

Among the new faces that shone in the Allied air triumph over the Somme, an especially youthful one stood out. Albert Ball was 19 years old when he reported during the build-up for the battle. One of the first times he fired the machine gun on his Bristol Scout he nearly shot himself down: Because of a faulty synchronizer, the bullets sawed his propeller almost in half. Ball switched to a Nieuport 16 and soon went on a three-month streak that eclipsed anything that had yet been seen in air combat. Between the beginning of July and the end of September he brought down 30 enemy planes, to outdistance both Boelcke and Guynemer and to become, for a time, the most successful pilot in the War. For his exploits he earned the Distinguished Service Order and the adulation of a British nation that until now had been slow to make a public fuss over its pilots.

Ball had some practical preparation for his hero's role. At his family's home in Nottingham, young Albert had taken over the lawn-tennis court to practice pistol shooting, at which he became expert. He had experimented with a succession of engines and radio equipment that he brought home to his workshop, an old shed behind the house; by the time he was 17 he was managing a small brass foundry and electrical contracting shop.

Ball's fighting style combined parts of Guynemer's and Hawker's, with some original moves of his own. Like Nungesser and other French aces, Ball was an individualist. He hated formation flying and often broke away to fight his own battles. Some days he ignored the squadron altogether to prowl alone for quarry.

Like Guynemer, Ball became a fuss-budget about his plane and its armament. He adjusted and readjusted the gun mount, a curved track called a Foster mount that allowed the Lewis gun to be swung into position either for reloading or for firing upward. He had the plane

Made in France to serve the Allies

France produced some of the finest—and certainly the most widely used—aircraft of World War I. Planes built or designed in France stocked not only the French escadrilles but the air forces of Belgium, Italy, Russia, Great Britain and—beginning in 1917—the United States.

The two-seater Breguet 14.B2 *(bottom)* was France's workhorse bomber. It was built largely of canvas-covered duralumin, a material relatively new to aviation, and had the advantage of dual controls. The nimble Nieuport 17 fighter, shown at right with a synchronized machine gun, was introduced in early 1916 and helped to wrest control of the air from the German Fokkers. Later the sturdy Spad 13 *(below),* built by the Société pour l'Aviation et ses Dé-rivés, served the aces of several nations. France's René Fonck notched the majority of his 75 victories in a Spad 13, as did America's Eddie Rickenbacker most of his 26.

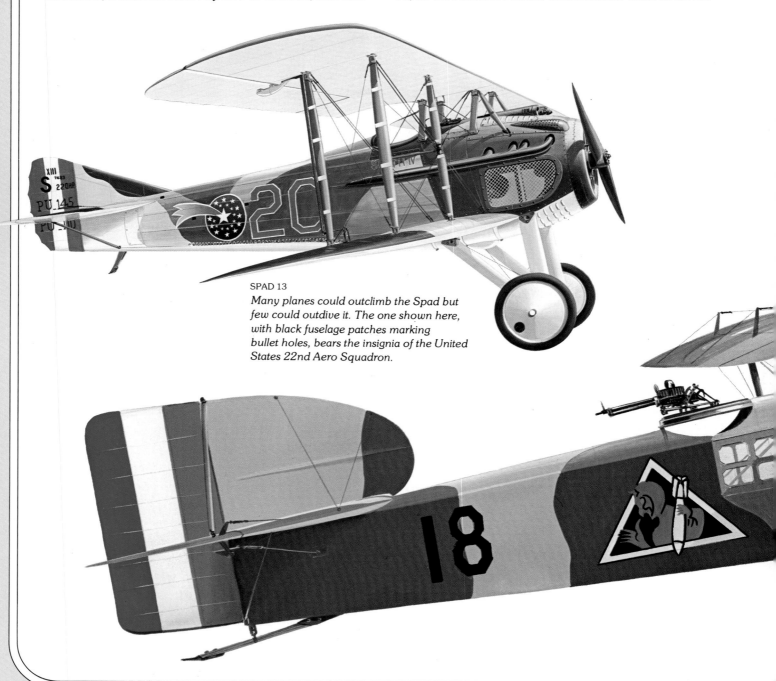

SPAD 13
Many planes could outclimb the Spad but few could outdive it. The one shown here, with black fuselage patches marking bullet holes, bears the insignia of the United States 22nd Aero Squadron.

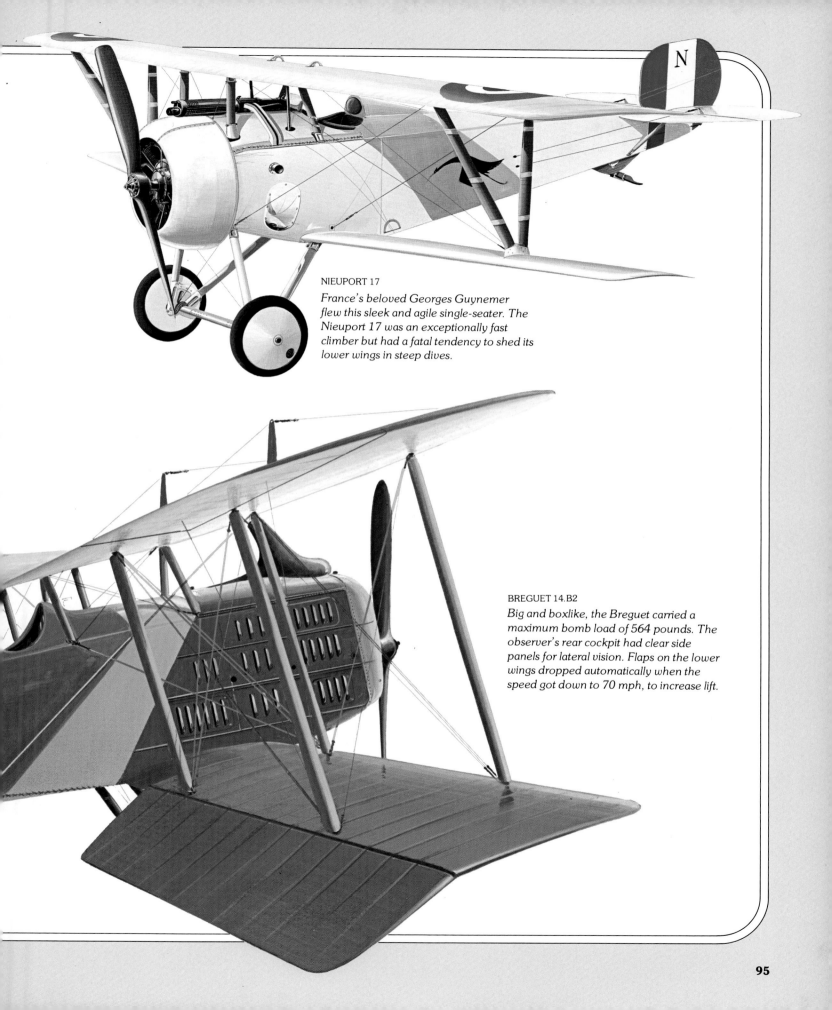

NIEUPORT 17

France's beloved Georges Guynemer flew this sleek and agile single-seater. The Nieuport 17 was an exceptionally fast climber but had a fatal tendency to shed its lower wings in steep dives.

BREGUET 14.B2

Big and boxlike, the Breguet carried a maximum bomb load of 564 pounds. The observer's rear cockpit had clear side panels for lateral vision. Flaps on the lower wings dropped automatically when the speed got down to 70 mph, to increase lift.

modified so that during the crucial seconds of engagement it could fly steadily "hands off," allowing him to use both hands on the machine gun. He was the first to attach a mirror to the wing above his cockpit so he could see behind him without having to swivel his head; the arrangement was later copied by many Allied and German pilots.

In his modified Nieuport, Ball became the ultimate exponent of Lanoe Hawker's maxim: Attack everything. His aggressiveness often got him into trouble: He was shot down half a dozen times. One of those occasions occurred at the end of August 1916. Ball had set forth alone in his Nieuport to challenge German fighters based at Cambrai. When they rose to intercept him, Ball dived straight into their midst, scattering them into an array of individual targets for his Lewis gun. Two of Ball's prey fluttered to earth out of control. But the Germans fought back and caught Ball in a vicious cross fire that eventually put his engine out of commission. Ammunition spent, the frustrated Ball drew his pistol and fired a parting round at his foes before gliding across Allied lines and safely crash-landing his crippled plane.

In exploits like these, Ball developed his own method of scoring kills. Whenever possible he tried to maneuver under a German's fuselage. Then, pulling down the gun's breech, he would fire upward from as close as 10 yards, sometimes swinging his plane from side to side to rake the enemy's bottom.

Curiously, Ball's achievements in the air never seemed to put him at ease with his squadron mates. He did not billet with the other men. Instead he lived by himself in a wooden shack he called his "dear old hut," out behind his squadron's farthermost hangar. Between missions he dug for hours in the vegetable garden adjoining his hut, planted with seeds he had asked his family to send. At night, instead of roistering with the other pilots, he would stay in the hut, listening to his windup gramophone or playing on a violin.

This private and deeply emotional young man could never make up his mind how he felt about being a professional warrior. One day he would describe the German flier as "a good chap trying to do his best. Nothing makes me feel more rotten than to see them go down." Another time he would recount with relish how he had strafed a disabled plane "to make certain of the passengers."

His letter to his sister of August 24, 1916, was filled with passages of exhilaration and bravado:

"Cheerio dears.

"Really, I am having too much luck for a boy. Met twelve Huns.

"No. 1 fight. I attacked and fired, bringing the machine down just outside a village. All crashed up.

"No. 2 fight. I attacked under the machine. Hun went down in flames.

"No. 3 fight. I attacked. Machine went down and crashed on a housetop.

"I only got hit 11 times in the wings, so I returned and got more ammunition. This time luck was not all on the spot. I was met by 14

Eyewitness art by a bombardier

Lieutenant Henri Farré, an observer-bombardier with the French air corps, carried a sketch pad with him everywhere he went—even into the air. His sketches, which he later committed to canvas, constitute an eyewitness record of the air war that, as Farré said, "was not only painted but lived by me on the different fronts of France."

Often the record was a somber one. The two paintings that are shown here describe the death of one of Farré's fellow aviators, killed by enemy bullets while returning from a bombing mission over Germany in 1915.

The death in 1915 of Captain Albert Féquant is portrayed in these two paintings. Above, he hangs mortally wounded from the observer's cockpit of his Voisin biplane. Below, the pilot offers a last salute as Féquant's body is lowered from the plane.

Huns, about 15 miles over their side. My windscreen was hit in four places, mirror broken, the spar of the left wing broken, also engine ran out of petrol.

"Oh, la, la. Topping, isn't it?"

But on another occasion Ball wrote (perhaps more honestly): "I do so want to leave all this beastly killing for a time."

By the end of September, these shifting moods had settled into a case of pilot fatigue, a phenomenon that was so new that air service doctors had not yet given it a name and so subtle in its symptoms that few pilots recognized its onset.

One American who flew with the British described the cumulative effects of weeks of flying daily missions on poor rations and insufficient sleep: "You're tense at the beginning, then you reach the stage of being very cool and collected. You think you're a pretty good shot and a damned good pilot, and 'it's going to take someone a hell of a lot better to shoot me down.' " After the euphoria came the fatigue, slower reflexes and a foolhardiness that made fliers take unnecessary risks. The cure was a change of pace, but only occasionally were overworked pilots grounded, granted extended leave or reassigned to the rear.

Ball was lucky. He sensed that something was wrong—he had been taking too many chances of late—and asked his squadron commander to send him home for a while. A few days later Ball received word that, although he was only 20, he had been promoted to the rank of captain. Then he went home, to receive the Distinguished Service Order personally from King George V and to recuperate during a tour of safe and restful duty in England.

The final lift for the Allies during their season of success in the air came from a high-spirited group of American volunteers. Originally their squadron was known as the *Escadrille Américaine*—until the German Ambassador in Washington complained about such blatant partisanship on the part of supposed neutrals. Thereafter they were called the Lafayette Escadrille, for the noble Frenchman who had fought under George Washington in the American Revolution. From the escadrille's inception in April 1916, thirty-eight Americans served in it at various times. They were not the only Americans to fly for France; another 172 volunteers served in the French air service and, though they were scattered among many units, they were known collectively as the Lafayette Flying Corps. The Americans wrought only modest damage on the Germans—in its nearly 20 months of combat the Lafayette Escadrille was credited with 57 victories—but their presence at the front tied the United States closer to the Allies and carried the promise of far greater American help to come.

The Lafayette Escadrille arrived at Cachy, near the Somme, in October and the Americans immediately established themselves as the most stylish hosts on the Western Front. The fliers' first look at Cachy's drab lodgings sent two of them racing to Paris; there they acquired a truck

This French pilot's certificate, typical of the credentials carried by airmen in case of capture, was issued to Serbian pilot Sava Mikitch. Lacking facilities, Serbia sent many prospective fliers to France for training.

Signature du Titulaire:

N°. du Brevet: 1839

and piled it high with iron stoves, pots, pans and tableware. On their way back they abducted from a neighboring regiment a French chef who had once worked at the Ritz in New York.

Soon French and British aviators were arriving in a stream, enjoying not only the food but the noisy, incessant dice and poker games and a gramophone that played an endless assortment of ragtime, fox trots and operas. (The records also included Hawaiian music, which the unit's French commanding officer, Captain Georges Thénault, described as "strange melodies played by a sort of banjo called a Ukelele.") The visitors were equally charmed by the Americans' tawny mascots, a pair of lion cubs named Whiskey and Soda, bought in Paris, which romped freely around the base.

Most of all, the Allied veterans liked the free and easy style of the Americans themselves. The particular favorite of the Storks was a square-cut American of French parentage named Raoul Lufbery. His mates had only recently bailed Lufbery out of a jail in Chartres, where he had been incarcerated for knocking out the teeth of a railway employee unwise enough to lay hands on him during an argument. Here was a man after the heart of Nungesser, who came calling on the escadrille. On one early visit the French ace, still recuperating from his latest wounds, scored a kill for the escadrille in a borrowed Nieuport that he took aloft to show the newcomers how it was done.

Raoul Lufbery had traveled a long road to France and the escadrille. He had been a United States soldier in the Philippines, then a mechanic for a barnstorming pilot in India, China and Egypt. In 1914 he turned up in Paris with his pilot friend to enlist in the French Foreign Legion, the only option open to an American citizen who wanted to serve. And, like many other Legionnaires, he transferred to the air service and went to the front as a mechanic. By the following October, Lufbery had finished pilot training and was flying regular bombing sorties.

For most members of the Lafayette Escadrille the route to the Western Front had been simpler, if sometimes frustratingly slow. The brothers Kiffin and Paul Rockwell came from Asheville, North Carolina. One of their forebears had fought in George Washington's army along with the Marquis de Lafayette, and the Rockwells had written the French consul in New Orleans to say that fighting for France would be their way of sustaining the republican ideal. Amateur flier William Thaw, also a Legion volunteer, came from a wealthy Pittsburgh family. Victor Chapman, who had been doing graduate work in Paris, had retreated briefly to London with his vacationing parents when France mobilized, then returned to Paris to enlist. And student aviator Norman Prince paid his way from Prides Crossing, Massachusetts, with the specific idea of forming an American volunteer squadron.

Prince discussed his plan with other expatriates in Paris and with the French bureaucracy—though the latter would at first have none of it. They had just shot an English-speaking spy who had insinuated himself into the French air service by pretending to be an American volunteer.

But as France's war casualties climbed past two million early in 1916, the French government grew more willing to listen to anyone who wanted to help. Dr. Edmund L. Gros, an influential leader of the American volunteer ambulance service in Paris, also advocated the idea of a volunteer air squadron. Through Dr. Gros, the Americans eventually got their message through to a newly appointed Director of Aeronautics, who authorized the formation of a volunteer escadrille. Some Americans signed up in a spirit of adventure, others because they believed strongly in the ideals of the Allied cause and hoped to bring lasting peace to the world. Virtually all were self-sacrificing individualists who put aside comfortable lives to face the dangers of the infant air war.

An allotment of Nieuport fighters was earmarked for the Americans as soon as they had been trained. Some of the group, like Lufbery, had already joined the French air service and had acquired experience, at least in two-seaters; the others received standard French training. In April they were sent to a quiet sector at Luxeuil, where, theoretically, they could learn to handle their Nieuports in safety. Luxeuil proved to be safe enough—and as sybaritic a billet as any group of fighting men ever enjoyed.

The place had been a royal health spa in the reign of Louis XV and had lost none of its opulence. Natural hot-spring baths still bubbled into pink granite tubs. At the superb old inn where the pilots were billeted, Captain Thénault recalled dining on "delicious trout from a neighboring stream, fat chickens, game, hares, wild-fowl . . . carefully cooked and washed down with generous burgundy." All around Luxeuil fruit trees blossomed on grassy slopes covered by flowers of blue and yellow. In the near distance rose the snow-capped Vosges Mountains, their flanks, according to volunteer James McConnell, "bristling with a solid mass of giant pines, the myriads of glittering cascades tumbling downward through fairylike avenues of verdure."

Thénault and the volunteers were delighted, too, with the support provided them by both the French government and a group of generous Americans in Paris, including Dr. Gros and William K. Vanderbilt. "At first sight," according to James McConnell, the escadrille's ground personnel "seemed to outnumber the Nicaraguan army—mechanicians, chauffeurs, armorers, motorcyclists, telephonists, wireless operators, Red Cross stretcher bearers, clerks!" Outside the inn, cars adorned with brass head lamps awaited the pilots' personal use; inside, servants appeared at a clap of the hands. "I recalled the ancient custom," said McConnell, "of giving a man selected for the sacrifice a royal time of it before the appointed day."

His qualms were well founded. In their idyllic circumstances, the young Americans in the spring of 1916 flew their Nieuports on patrols that were more scenic than dangerous—until, after about a month, Kiffin Rockwell reported that he had actually shot down a German plane, a two-seated L.V.G., for the escadrille's first victory. "An observation post telephoned the news before Rockwell's return," recounted

戰激大上海

A martial vision from Japa

壯絕快絕英獨 （其四十九）戰亂畫報 歐洲大

A mighty air and sea battle between German and British forces is imagined in a fanciful 1915 Japanese lithograph. Japan, which as yet had almost no experience with military aviation, had joined the War on the Allied side in August of 1914. Its citizens, curious about events in the West, avidly purchased lithographs like this because news photographs were difficult to obtain and to reproduce.

McConnell, "and he had a great welcome. All Luxeuil smiled upon him—particularly the girls. But," added McConnell, "he couldn't stay to enjoy his popularity." The escadrille had been ordered to Verdun.

At Bar-le-Duc airfield, the Lafayette Escadrille was quartered in a commodious villa and the War still seemed a glorious lark. Handsome, high-minded Victor Chapman, whose avowed purpose had been to fight "for the cause of humanity, the most noble of all causes," wrote home that "this flying is much too romantic to be real modern war with all its horrors. Yesterday afternoon the sky was bright but full of those very thick fuzzy clouds like imaginary froth of gods or genii. At 3,000 metres one floated secure on a purple sea of mist. Met a flock of Nieuports, and saw across the way a squad of white-winged L.V.G. How like a game of prisoner's base it all is!"

But suddenly the War became less of a game for Chapman. His friends had long regarded him as too brave for his own good. On patrol with Thénault and two others one day, he was flying under strict orders to stay on the right bank of the River Meuse. But when German planes appeared on the left bank, Thénault reported, Chapman, "like a tiger, dashed at a group of them." Chapman's friends followed and extracted him from a swarm of Germans, but later that day he went up alone and came back with head wounds and a badly shot-up airplane. Chapman then demanded another plane and ignored orders to stay down while his wounds healed. A week later, alone and still bandaged, he charged five Fokkers and was shot down behind enemy lines, his plane crumpling in the air as it fell; his was the first combat death of World War I in a recognized unit of American fighting men.

The escadrille struck back in a whirl of combat that earned four victories apiece for Lufbery and Kiffin Rockwell. But then Rockwell, too, was gone, killed while flying so impulsively at a German two-seater that he put himself in the rear gunner's line of fire. Three weeks after Rockwell's death, Norman Prince, who, along with Dr. Gros and William Thaw, had persuaded French officials to organize the escadrille, died of injuries sustained when his Nieuport hit a power line after flying escort on a bombing raid. Prince had flown 122 sorties against enemy planes in less than six months at the front. He was officially credited with five kills, but his fellow officers attributed several more to him that were never reckoned in the official count.

Thus did the Americans become fully blooded in the summer of 1916 in what a contemporary report described as "the first great organized employment of aerial squadrons." These Allied squadrons, in the words of a disgruntled German general, had achieved "mastery of the air almost undisputed," and Boom Trenchard of the RFC could report with satisfaction that in a single autumn week "only 14 hostile machines crossed the line of the Fourth Army area, whereas something like 2,000 to 3,000 of our machines crossed the lines," destroying, among other targets, 521 heavy guns.

Proudly assessing France's performance, Captain Felix Brocard not-

Norman Prince learned to fly after graduating from Harvard, then helped to organize American volunteers into the Lafayette Escadrille. He shot down five German planes before his death in 1916.

A commemorative flag made for the Lafayette Escadrille and Flying Corps after the War bears the Escadrille's Indian-head emblem and stars representing the 65 members who died during the War.

ed that his Storks alone had engaged in 388 air battles, knocking down 72 planes. Brocard was especially pleased with Georges Guynemer, whom he praised as "my most brilliant Stork." That brilliance would by no means diminish. Guynemer in September had switched from his Nieuport to an even faster new fighter, the Spad 7. The name was an acronym for the manufacturer, the Société pour l'Aviation et ses Dérivés, and the plane carried a synchronized Vickers machine gun. Guynemer painted the name *Vieux Charles*—"old Charles"—on his Spad's fuselage and set out to earn a dividend on Brocard's tribute.

He got more than he bargained for. After bringing down three German planes with a brilliant display of close shooting, he was cruising back toward his own lines at 10,000 feet when a stray shot from French antiaircraft blew the fabric from his upper wing. The plane spun 5,000 feet before Guynemer managed to pull out and glide to a crash landing only 100 yards from the battery that had fired at him.

The French gunners were horrified. They had recognized the plane as it rushed toward the earth, and they thought they had just broken forever the Winged Sword of France. Then they saw the pale face and thin body of Guynemer rise from the wreckage of the Spad. His only injury was a badly gashed knee. The gunners ran to him and, despite the wound, tried to lift him to their shoulders in triumph. Then they began to sing—first one voice, then another and another, until all voices were singing together—a rousing chorus of the "Marseillaise." ～

Members of the Lafayette Escadrille, assembled for a photograph outside their barracks at Chaudun, France, are upstaged by their lion-cub mascots, Whiskey and Soda. Seated fourth from left is the Escadrille's French commanding officer, Captain Georges Thénault. Raoul Lufbery, the unit's top-ranking ace with 17 victories, is seated fourth from right.

Tribute to a gallant few

Their motives were many, and some, perhaps, naïve: adventure, glory, a simple urge, as one of them said, "to get into the scrap." But as Edwin Parsons said many years later of the Lafayette Escadrille, in which he served, "I don't know a single one of the boys who didn't have a deep-seated desire to help France."

The gallant gesture of the young Americans—and some of them indeed were little more than boys—touched an appreciative nerve among the French. After the War a joint Franco-American committee honored the volunteers with a permanent memorial, of which the stained-glass windows reproduced on these and the following pages are a part.

Between 1916 and 1918, when most—though not all—of them transferred to the United States Air Service, more than 200 Americans flew for France. Some served with the original Lafayette Escadrille while others formed the Lafayette Flying Corps and were scattered throughout the French air service. "They were fighting to get in," Parsons recalled. And once in, they fought well; all told, they were credited with 199 air victories. But the price was high: 63 of the Americans were killed in action. Two others died of illness and accident before the Armistice.

Most of the dead are buried at the Lafayette Escadrille Memorial near Versailles. Dedicated on the Fourth of July, 1928, the shrine is composed of a central arch of triumph flanked by colonnades, and a sanctuary or burial crypt. Light filters into the tomb through a series of 13 stained-glass windows, which were paid for by public subscription in France and America. Designed by an anonymous artist, they show the United States airmen in flight over the various sectors where they did battle.

In a tribute composed for the memorial, English poet Richard Le Gallienne wrote in part: "France of the many lovers, none than these / Hath brought you love of an intenser flame . . . / Their golden youth they gave, and here are laid / Deep in the arms of France for whom they died."

Escorted by a militant eagle, American planes are shown in symbolic flight across the Atlantic in this stained-glass window, entitled For Liberty, in the Lafayette Escadrille shrine near Paris.

An attack by the Lafayette Escadrille on hotly contested Hartmannswillerkopf mountain is portrayed in this triptych.

The Lafayette Flying Corps supports French tanks in this window depicting an Allied push against the Craonne plateau in 1917.

An eagle, representing the American presence, protects the French cathedral at Rheims, a frequent target of German bombers.

A swarm of aircraft dives on German positions near Château-Thierry, the scene of major American fighting in 1918.

107

Runway on the waves

From the moment that the flying machine showed signs of military usefulness, navies of the world sought ways to employ airplanes at sea. In a 1910 experiment American pilot Eugene Ely, in a Curtiss biplane, took off down a sloping ramp built above the foredeck of the cruiser U.S.S. *Birmingham*. The plane dipped so low that the tips of its propeller splintered against the water, yet Ely managed a safe landing ashore. Several months later, he set down successfully on the anchored battleship U.S.S. *Pennsylvania,* which had been outfitted with a level landing platform.

During the War, England's Navy pioneered the launching of planes at sea to bomb and scout the enemy—although with limited success. After its mission, a land plane launched from a ship had to choose between heading for shore or ditching near the ship. Seaplanes could be recovered in calm seas, but the ships that carried them steamed so slowly that, after stopping to hoist the planes from the water, they could not catch up with the fleet.

To solve that problem, the British converted a partially built light cruiser, H.M.S. *Furious,* into a seaplane carrier. With a top speed of 31½ knots, the *Furious (right)* was fast enough to overtake other ships after a retrieval.

Taking off from the forward deck of the *Furious* as it steamed into the wind was safe enough. Landing, on the other hand, appeared to be so risky that it was not even part of the Admiralty's plans for the ship. Then Squadron Commander E. H. Dunning, the ship's senior pilot, persuaded his superiors to let him try a landing; he would have to fly slowly alongside the ship, then sideslip deftly in front of the bridge and onto the deck. In August 1917, Dunning demonstrated that such a landing was possible, although extremely hazardous *(pages 112-115)*. A landing deck equipped with rudimentary arresting gear was built onto the stern of the *Furious* the following winter, but trial landings on it were largely unsuccessful.

However, the *Furious* still could launch its warplanes. On July 19, 1918, having slipped to within 80 miles of the German dirigible base at Tondern, it dispatched seven Sopwith Camels that destroyed two enemy airships on the ground. All but one of the pilots survived, either by ditching or by landing safely in Denmark.

Aboard H.M.S. Furious, a Sopwith 1½ Strutter is poised on the forward takeoff deck at left, protected from gusts by a fencelike collapsible windbreak. At right, a small airship used for scouting submarines has landed on the afterdeck. A rope barrier in front of the airship was originally installed to prevent landing airplanes from accidentally ramming the funnel.

Three Sopwith Camels are lined up on the deck of H.M.S. Furious. The hatch in the foreground leads to a hangar deck that held eight planes.

A wheeled trolley (foreground) supported the pontoons of seaplanes during their takeoff runs. It was left behind as the planes lifted off.

Attempting to land on the deck of H.M.S. Furious, Squadron Commander E. H. Dunning approaches in a Sopwith Pup at a relative speed little faster than that of the ship. Fellow officers advance to slow the plane to a stop by grabbing handles attached to its wings and tail.

Commander Dunning emerges from the cockpit of his plane as officers and crew of the Furious crowd around to congratulate him for the first successful landing on a ship under way on August 2, 1917.

After two successful landings, Dunning made a third attempt, in gusty weather. Above, officers chase his plane as it touches down, far along the deck. Seconds earlier, realizing his approach was faulty, Dunning had tried to regain altitude for a second try, but the engine failed to respond, and when the plane hit the deck, the right tire blew out.

Unable to grab Dunning's plane in time, the flight crew watches helplessly as it plunges over the side. Before it could be retrieved, Squadron Commander Dunning had drowned in the cockpit.

4

The year of the Red Baron

At a sandy German airfield near Kovel on the scorched plains of western Russia, Lieutenant Manfred von Richthofen responded to a knock at his quarters door on an August morning in 1916. He opened it to find "a big man wearing the Pour le Mérite" standing there. The visitor was Captain Oswald Boelcke and his presence rendered Richthofen speechless. "I didn't dare think," he wrote later, "that he might have selected me to be one of his pupils." But that is exactly what Boelcke wanted. He had been ordered back to the Western Front to organize a new fighting unit in a German Air Service that was about to be drastically reorganized. Boelcke, moreover, had been given a free hand to select the pilots he wanted, and Richthofen, once he recovered from the surprise, "almost hugged him" for joy at being chosen. Three days later Richthofen was riding a train westward toward "the most wonderful time of my life."

It was a fateful encounter. Boelcke was more than his nation's leading ace; he was establishing himself as a pioneer air tactician, a teacher and combat leader of legendary stature. Richthofen, still an obscure pilot with a single unconfirmed victory to his credit, would become his disciple extraordinary, eventually surpassing the master as a nemesis of Allied fliers. Together, teacher and pupil would be instrumental in lifting the German Air Service from its doldrums, and Richthofen would preside over the finest hours of a sustained German resurgence in the air.

The German military machine, which had begun the year 1916 with such great promise, had by late summer sunk close to disaster. Though German troops had surrendered little ground to the continuing Allied drive along the Somme, the cost of their effort was approaching 500,000 casualties. In the air, Allied offensive action continued to hold the imperial air service in a state of what a senior German commander called "complete inferiority." In early August Germany had only about 250 operational aircraft at the Somme, just half the Allied total. Frustrated at Verdun and staggered at the Somme, the Chief of the German General Staff, Erich von Falkenhayn, resigned on August 28.

Falkenhayn's successor, Field Marshal Paul von Hindenburg, and his new quartermaster general, Erich Ludendorff, prepared a plan to increase the production of German airplanes and to shift the bulk of German air power from Verdun, where the offensive had been suspended, to the embattled Somme. By the end of 1916 some 33 new pursuit squadrons—called *Jagdstaffeln,* or *Jastas* or *Staffeln* for

With his cap at a rakish tilt and the Blue Max at his collar, Germany's Manfred von Richthofen radiates knightly confidence. The German government proudly distributed thousands of copies of this photograph of its Ace of Aces.

short—were to be in action at the front, each equipped with 14 new planes. Creation of the *Jastas* was the first visible step in a sweeping reorganization, which, as Count von Moltke had urged years before, united the Air Service "in one authority" as a separate branch of the Army. General Ernst von Hoeppner was named overall air commander with the experienced Lieutenant Colonel von der Lieth-Thomsen as his chief of staff; together they set German air strategy on an aggressive new course. No longer would German planes be confined to flying defensive patrols behind their own lines, nor would they fly alone. Henceforth, Hoeppner said, large formations of German fighters must be trained to operate "as a single tactical unit."

Oswald Boelcke had been assigned *Jagdstaffel 2* and was accorded the honor of sitting between Hindenburg and Ludendorff at a head-quarters luncheon. To him, the new strategy meant a realization of ideas he had been sending up through the chain of command for nearly a year. By the end of August he had assembled the first of his chosen pilots at Bertincourt and set about training them in the Boelcke image. For three weeks, while the *Jasta* waited for its new planes to arrive, Boelcke often flew alone—and with a vengeance, adding six victims to the string that had been interrupted in June. After each flight the fledg-lings would crowd around, asking if he had been successful. "Do I have a black chin?" he replied. And usually he did, from the smoke of his machine gun. It meant that he had scored again.

Richthofen, like the other fliers, worshipped Boelcke, though he was only one year younger than the great ace. "He shot one or two English-men for breakfast every day," Manfred bragged. Boelcke would explain in professional detail to the less-experienced pilots how he worked: The Nieuport, for example, was "very fast and agile. It generally loses height in prolonged turning action. Attack from behind if possible and at close range."

"Everything Boelcke told us was Gospel," wrote Richthofen, and Boelcke enjoyed the attentiveness of his men. "They are like young puppies in their zeal," he said, and when asked which of his puppies might mature into an outstanding fighter pilot, he nodded toward Richthofen: "That is the man."

But Boelcke had no interest in individual heroes. He insisted that the *Jasta* learn to function as a team, flying in tight formation with every plane in its place. "Everything depends on sticking together when the *Staffel* goes into battle," he said sternly. "It does not matter who actually scores the victory as long as the *Staffel* wins."

On September 16, *Jasta 2* received the new biplanes it had been waiting for: the sleek Albatros D.II, with a light but sturdy plywood frame, 160 horsepower in-line Mercedes engine and twin Spandau machine guns. The excited fliers were convinced that with this plane they could outclimb and outshoot anything in the sky. The next morn-ing, after test-firing their machine guns and listening to Boelcke's final instructions, *Jasta 2* followed him into the air. "It was a gloriously fine

A master warrior's rules for winning

At his superiors' behest, Oswald Boelcke drew on his experience in combat to write these concise rules for fighter pilots, who ob-served them until the end of the War as the official doctrine of the German Air Service.

BOELCKE'S DICTA

Try to secure advantages before attacking. If possible keep the sun behind you.

Always carry through an attack when you have started it.

Fire only at close range and only when your opponent is properly in your sights.

Always keep your eye on your opponent, and never let yourself be deceived by ruses.

In any form of attack it is essential to assail your opponent from behind.

If your opponent dives on you, do not try to evade his onslaught, but fly to meet it.

When over the enemy's lines, never forget your own line of retreat.

Attack on principle in groups of four or six. When the fight breaks up into a series of sin-gle combats, take care that several do not go for one opponent.

This silver medal depicting Oswald Boelcke in profile commemorates his death in a mid-air collision in October 1916.

day," recalled Richthofen. "We had just arrived at the front when we recognized a hostile squadron. Boelcke was of course the first to see it. It was clear to all of us that we had to pass our first examination under the eyes of our beloved leader."

The pups had learned their lessons well. In the melee that followed, every German knocked a British plane to the ground. "My first Englishman!" exulted Richthofen. He celebrated by ordering from Berlin a small silver cup engraved with the date of his initial success as a member of *Jasta 2*.

A week later Richthofen was able to order a second cup and the following week a third. He also became a determined collector of souvenirs. It was usually possible to track down fallen enemy aircraft, and from his second victim Richthofen took the machine gun, which had been hit and put out of commission by Richthofen's own gun. After that it was serial numbers, pistols, propeller fragments—anything that could be salvaged from a fallen machine. He sent it all home to his mother and she faithfully arranged it in Manfred's old room in the family's great house at Schweidnitz.

It was a heady time for a young German who had grown up to a centuries-old tradition of service to the fatherland, but who had found the first two years of his war more frustrating than glorious.

Born May 2, 1892, at Breslau, Prussia, Manfred von Richthofen was the eldest of three brothers in a family whose ancestral credentials as barons came from the hand of Frederick the Great. He grew up riding, hunting and swimming on various family estates, and then, after cadet and officer training, became a lieutenant in a regiment of uhlan cavalry. He cut a handsome figure, with his silky blond hair, finely chiseled face and erect carriage, and he whipped his horse over steeplechase courses with sufficient dash to win the coveted Kaiser's Prize.

Of the outbreak of war he wrote solemnly, "It is in the blood of every German to rush to meet the enemy." It was during the early part of the War that cavalryman Richthofen penetrated so far into Poland on a mission that he was nearly captured by Russian soldiers. Transferred to the Western Front, he soon rushed into a French ambush, losing most of the 15 uhlans in his patrol. "If I live through this war," he wrote in one of many letters home, "I will have more luck than sense." The mud-clogged Western Front, with its trenches and barbed wire, was no place for a cavalryman, and for the next eight months Richthofen drew a series of dreary assignments in which he described himself variously as a "base-hog" and a "cellar hero." He finally struck bottom with duty as a supply officer, and although he later denied it, he was reported to have complained to his commanding officer that "I did not go to war to gather cheese and eggs." In any case, his petition for transfer was approved, and at the end of May 1915 he was reassigned, this time to the Air Service.

"There is nothing finer for a young cavalry officer," Richthofen wrote, "than flying off on a hunt." But the young cavalier also displayed

The Baron's triple-decker

Baron Manfred von Richthofen scored the final 21 of his 80 victories in Fokker Dr.I triplanes, including the one shown here in cutaway. Introduced in late 1917, the Dr.I had not only three wings but a supplementary airfoil on the undercarriage. These features enabled the diminutive plane (length: 18 feet, 11 inches; wingspan: 23 feet, 7 inches) to outclimb and outturn almost any contemporary Allied aircraft. But the small engine, an Oberursel of only 110 horsepower, limited top speed to 103 miles per hour.

Nevertheless, in a dogfight a skilled aviator flying the agile triplane usually enjoyed the advantage. He could evade pursuit by turning tightly, and once on his quarry's tail, he could rarely be shaken off except by a high-speed dive. If the duel dipped to treetop level, an Allied pilot had only one course of escape: to zigzag away as fast as his plane would fly. Any attempt to turn or to climb merely closed the distance between him and the Fokker's guns.

The one tactic likely to defeat a Dr.I was to dive from above—the approach used by a Canadian pilot in the battle that cost Richthofen his life.

The control column of the Fokker Dr.I had convenient firing buttons for the machine guns—mounted directly in front of the cockpit—and a remote control for the throttle. But cockpit instruments were sparse. Besides fuel and oil gauges (not visible here), a pilot had only a tachometer and a compass to help fly the plane.

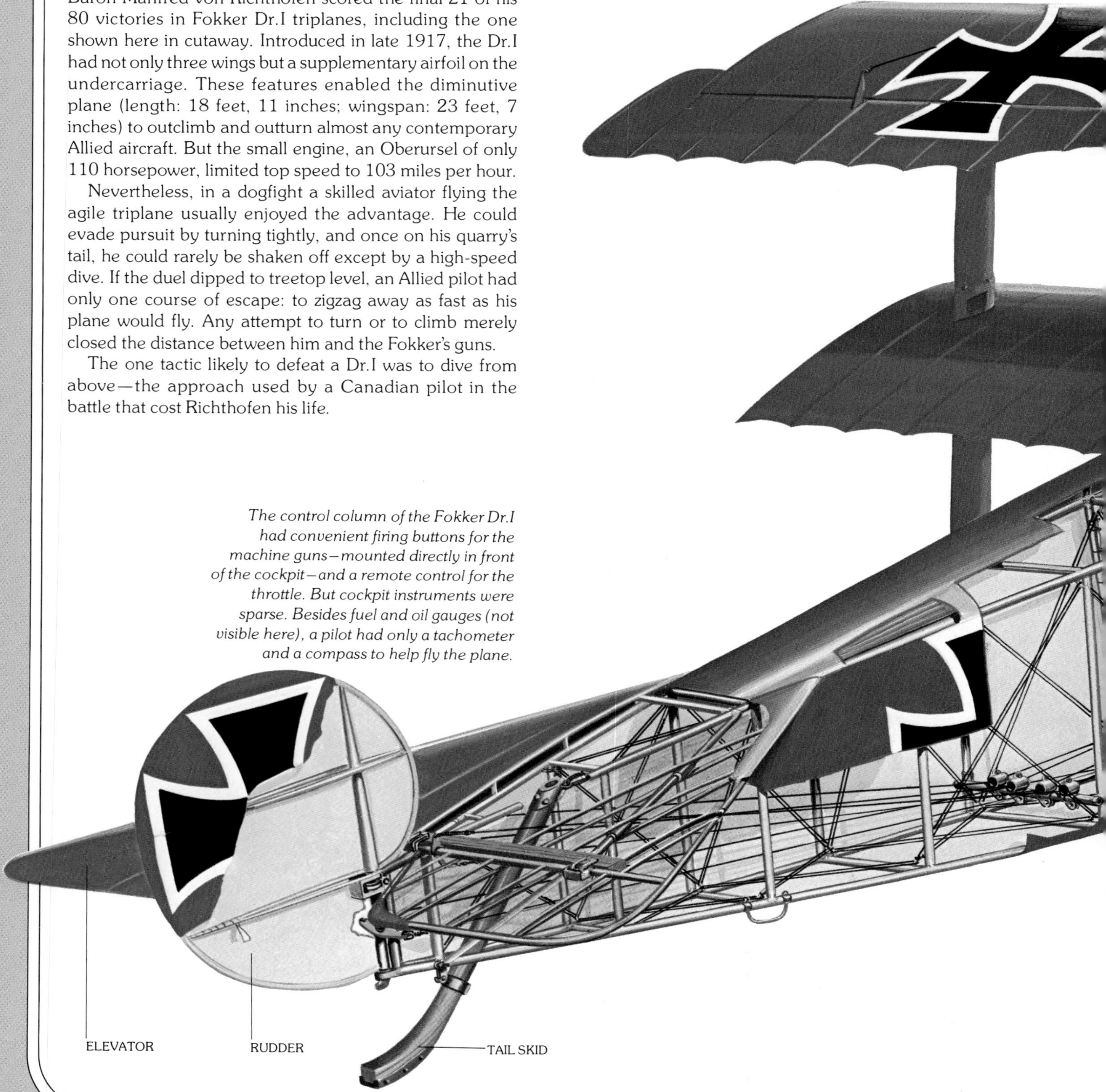

ELEVATOR   RUDDER   TAIL SKID

THROTTLE   CONTROL COLUMN   WING RIB   WING SPAR

AILERON

OIL/FUEL TANK

ROTARY ENGINE

WING STRUT

MAGAZINE

RUDDER BAR

TACHOMETER   COMPASS   UNDERCARRIAGE AIRFOIL   WING-TIP SKID

a self-deprecating sense of humor. Describing the first time he climbed into a flying machine, he reported that he "found it impossible to make myself heard by the pilot. If I took out a piece of paper, it disappeared. My flying helmet slipped off. My muffler dropped off. My jacket was not sufficiently buttoned. In short, I was miserable." All this, and the idling plane had not even left the ground.

The young baron persevered, however, and soon became a qualified observer, serving first on the Russian Front and later in Belgium with Germany's first long-range bombing unit, the Ostend Carrier Pigeons. Then a chance meeting with Oswald Boelcke in a railroad dining car in October of 1915 inspired him to apply for pilot training. Boelcke, already becoming famous, encouraged him to try for fighters. Richthofen's first efforts as a pilot were unpromising. Asked if he was ready to fly alone, he wanted to answer "I am too afraid." But such a response, he knew, "could not come from a defender of the Fatherland. Therefore, I had to swallow my cowardice and sit in the machine." On this first solo flight, he crash-landed; on his first pilot's exam, he failed. But on Christmas Day he passed his third and final examination and now, a year after that casual meeting with Boelcke, he was discovering that he shared his mentor's special gift for air combat. On October 16, 1916, Richthofen shot down his sixth enemy plane. The next day Boelcke shot down his 35th; the week before, he had regained his position as the War's leading ace from Britain's Albert Ball.

Boelcke and his star pupil were not alone. Between mid-September and mid-October, *Jasta 2* shot down some 40 Allied fliers. Other *Jastas* were adding to the score. German records for September and October indicated that the Allies lost 211 machines to 39 for the Germans. Allied control of the air over the Somme had been broken—"due in no slight measure," declared a jubilant General von Hoeppner, "to Boelcke and the *Jagdstaffel* he led." Boelcke had stopped calling his pilots pups. "They are really splendid, clever gentlemen, my *Staffel*," he conceded. And though sometimes he had to "turn my heavy batteries on them and deal out severe criticism," their deep respect for him never wavered. The men of *Jasta 2* showed no sign of slowing down. Boelcke himself brought down five more planes in late October for a total of 40. But the Germans would pay a bitter price for their victories.

On the gusty gray afternoon of October 28, five of *Jasta 2's* planes took off from their new field at Lagnicourt to support an infantry attack. Boelcke and his close friend Erwin Böhme were wing to wing in the formation, with Richthofen above them. Reaching the front, the Germans engaged two British fighters. Guns blazing, wheeling through the sky, Böhme and Boelcke maneuvered to dodge an enemy plane as it cut in front of them with Richthofen in close pursuit. Almost imperceptibly, Boelcke's left wing brushed the undercarriage of Böhme's plane. Boelcke's Albatros began to spiral toward the ground, the left wing ripped away, and what was left of the plane fell heavily to earth.

Oswald Boelcke was dead, but his spirit would live on among young

German airmen, who were told at his graveside a few days later that henceforth their personal motto must be: "I will be a Boelcke."

That seemed a tall order. But Manfred von Richthofen, for one, set out to become the equal of his fallen leader, in whose honor *Jasta 2* was renamed *Jagdstaffel Boelcke.* By November 9, Richthofen had brought down his eighth enemy plane, noting in disappointment that it was too bad a man no longer received the Blue Max for eight victories, as Boelcke and Immelmann had. Then, two weeks later, Richthofen got a prize of a different sort.

On patrol out of Lagnicourt, he was attacked by a British D.H.2, which maneuvered so adroitly that Richthofen immediately realized he must be facing one of the enemy's best. The two adversaries circled skillfully, each trying to gain the advantage and squeeze off a fatal burst into the other plane's rear. The D.H.2 could turn more tightly, but Richthofen's Albatros had the edge in speed. Banking steeply as they flew, the pilots had a clear view of each other; once the Englishman waved cheerfully at his German foe.

The British pilot threw his plane into a succession of looping maneuvers, its gun chattering, the bullets whizzing close to Richthofen's Albatros. Then, his fuel evidently running low, the Englishman abandoned the duel and struck out on a desperate zigzag flight for home. Richthofen followed in tight pursuit and, just short of the British lines, brought down his quarry with a bullet through the brain. A short time later, he learned that his victim was Major Lanoe Hawker, spirited commander of No. 24 Squadron and holder of the Victoria Cross.

Richthofen's triumph over one of Britain's first air heroes typified the resurgence of German arms. As 1916 drew to a close, Allied assaults at the Somme came to an end at a cost of more than a million casualties on both sides. More than a third of a million Frenchmen had fallen at Verdun. On the Eastern Front, a great Russian offensive had collapsed after costing 1,000,000 Russian casualties; the Czar's Army was both battered and angry.

Meanwhile, German plane makers were upgrading the new *Jagdstaffeln* not only with an improved Albatros, the D.II, but also with dependable D-type Halberstadt fighter planes. And by January 1917 an even more advanced Albatros, the D.III—with a faster rate of climb and better high-altitude performance—was reaching Germany's frontline airfields.

In the same month, Manfred von Richthofen became his nation's number one living pilot, downing his 16th enemy plane. In mid-January the Kaiser bestowed on him the Pour le Mérite he had been waiting for, and he was chosen to command his own fighter unit, *Jagdstaffel 11.*

The medal seemed the better bargain of the two. *Jasta 11* had been in action almost as long as *Jasta Boelcke,* but it had only one unconfirmed victory to its credit. The new commander took it on himself to improve that dismal record: His first time in the air with his new unit, Richthofen scored his 17th kill.

The eagle subduing its foe on both the Naval Victory Trophy at top and the Honor Goblet at left symbolizes the triumph of a German pilot. The less-common naval trophy was won by Lieutenant Wolfram Eisenlohr for sinking a Russian destroyer. The goblet was presented to Lieutenant Ernst Hess, who scored 17 victories before his death in 1917.

Richthofen brought to his command the wisdom that Boelcke had bequeathed him, together with his own sense of mission. Between flights he would sit with his pilots and, in arm-waving discussions, show them what they should have done. Two in particular, Kurt Wolff and Karl Allmenröder, learned so well that in time they scored 33 and 30 victories respectively, and each earned his own Blue Max.

A personal mystique began to grow around Richthofen, due mostly to his success in individual combat and as a flight leader—but due also to the spectacular color of his airplane. Deciding that his Albatros should stand out in the eyes of friend and foe alike, he had it painted a startling red. Almost at once the blood-red plane became famous on both sides of the lines. Allied pilots who had to face it coined a French name for it: *le Diable Rouge*—"the Red Devil." There were rumors in one British squadron that the red plane must be piloted by a German Joan of Arc; only a woman would fly in such a garishly painted machine. German newspapers wrote that a British killer squadron had been formed whose

A photograph taken from the front cockpit of a Letord three-seater shows the gunner poised at twin Lewis machine guns while the pilot squints into a rearview mirror (center foreground) supported by cables.

sole mission was to bring down the red machine. The reward would be £5,000 for the man who did it. Richthofen wondered jovially if he could collect the prize if instead he shot down the whole British squadron—and during February and March of 1917 he did destroy, if not quite a squadron, 10 more British planes.

All this was particularly inspiring to a second Richthofen who arrived at the front fresh from flight school without a single hour of combat experience in fighters. His name was Lothar, and he had been assigned to *Jasta 11* at the insistence of his older brother, who protectively ordered Lothar to fly close behind him on his first mission "to observe what we did." Lothar was an apt pupil; on his third flight he peeled away from the formation and expertly blasted his first British plane out of the sky. "My heart leaped with joy," wrote Manfred.

Germany needed replacements who learned so quickly, for the first weeks of spring promised to be critical on the Western Front. The whole German forward wall was being pulled back to a shortened, heavily fortified position that became known to the Allies as the Hindenburg Line and to the Germans as the Siegfried Line. For the move to succeed, the Germans had to keep control of the air until their troops were safely off the roads and settled into their newly prepared positions.

During the last days of March, the air grew acrid with smoke from burning towns and bridges as the withdrawing Germans put the torch to anything that might be useful to the enemy. The Allies moved into the vacated zone. Hundreds of British fliers, piloting planes generally inferior to the new generation of German machines, came with a rush—many of them to their deaths. "We did not relinquish the air to the Englishmen," Richthofen declared, and thereafter British airmen would remember Bloody April of 1917 as the worst single period of the War.

For Richthofen the month's carnage started early on the morning of April 2, when his personal score stood at 31. As he lay abed in his quarters at Douai, his orderly rushed in and announced: "Sir, the English are here." Seeing that British planes were indeed circling overhead, Richthofen dressed quickly and scrambled to his red Albatros. Once aloft, he attacked one of the "impertinent fellows" and sent him crashing into a cluster of houses. The baron then returned to his quarters to shave and brush his hair.

Later that morning, Richthofen had a visit from Werner Voss, a former comrade in *Jasta Boelcke*. Voss was a free spirit who frequently lounged around the airdrome with shaggy wool socks pulled up over his trouser legs, his cap askew and his hands thrust in the pockets of an oil-smeared uniform. But in the air he wore his best tunic and a fresh silk shirt so that he could, as he cheerfully remarked, play the gentleman with the ladies of Paris if he should be shot down and captured. Voss's casual manner belied his fighting talent: Just the day before, he had scored his 23rd kill, making him second only to Richthofen among German pilots. That afternoon, with Voss flying close by as escort, Richthofen notched his 33rd victory—and ordered his 33rd silver cup.

Resolute knights of the fatherland

Of Germany's aces, the 11 on these pages ranked closest to Manfred von Richthofen *(page 116),* whose 80 victories were unsurpassed. None of them except Richthofen's brother Lothar shared his aristocratic background. The others were sons of soldiers and foresters, businessmen, teachers and doctors. Yet each in his own way matched the baron's ferocious singleness of purpose.

Rudolf Berthold became known as the Iron Knight; he flew combat missions with a suppurating wound that left him nearly crazed with pain. Franz Büchner once attacked a formation of eight British planes and brought down four. And Ernst Udet, to prove his bravery to himself and to a doubting father, eventually shot down more enemy planes than any German flier except Richthofen himself.

WERNER VOSS's flying skill was considered unparalleled by his foes. At his death he had 48 victories.

OSWALD BOELCKE scored his 40 victories in a 16-month period ended by his accidental death in 1916.

FRITZ RUMEY (45 victories) was among the few noncommissioned officers who became aces.

RUDOLF BERTHOLD (44 victories) was strangled with his own Blue Max by German Communists in 1920.

PAUL BÄUMER, who entered the Air Service as a dentist's assistant, ended the War with 43 victories.

LOTHAR VON RICHTHOFEN came out of the War as a convalescent with 40 victories. He was killed in an airplane crash in 1922.

ERNST UDET (62 victories) survived the War but committed suicide in 1941.

ERICH LOEWENHARDT (53 victories) had been declared physically unfit for the infantry.

FRANZ BÜCHNER (40 victories) established a German record by downing six Allied planes in one day.

JOSEF JACOBS (41 victories) fought to a stalemate such aces as Guynemer and Nungesser.

Once during the following fortnight he knocked down three planes on a single day—and his brother Lothar brought down a pair. Other *Jasta 11* fliers scored eight more victories that day.

In their season of triumph, Germany's fighting men received ominous news. The United States, inflamed by the sinking of its ships by German submarines, had declared war on Germany on April 6, 1917, and some American politicians were threatening to "darken the skies of Europe" with an armada of 20,000 airplanes. At about the same time British guns unleashed a terrible barrage to cover an assault on the Hindenburg Line at Arras. But German machine gunners scythed the fields until the tommies and their Canadian comrades stopped coming, and from Russia came news that more than balanced, for now, the prospect of American intervention. The Czar had abdicated in March, and despite the pledge of Russia's new government to keep fighting, the behemoth of the Eastern Front plainly was tottering. As for darkening the skies anywhere, the United States fleet of fewer than 250 military aircraft, none of them fit for combat, made that threat seem remote indeed.

The sky above Western Europe belonged to Germany that spring. And the German who cast the largest shadow by far was Manfred von Richthofen. At mid-April he had scored 45 victories—surpassing both Guynemer's total of 36 and the 40 of Boelcke. He had also become a bit less visible. His pilots had convinced him that one red plane represented too tempting a target, and now every plane in *Jasta 11* was painted a brilliant red—though all but Manfred's had some parts splashed with other hues; Lothar's tail, for instance, was a bright yellow.

By the end of Bloody April, Manfred had contributed 21 victories to Germany's bag of 150 British planes for the month. His career score stood at 52, and he was ready for a furlough—which he began on May 1, leaving Lothar in temporary command of *Jasta 11*. Lothar responded a week later by downing yet another Englishman—who may have been Captain Albert Ball.

The British ace had returned to the front in the midst of Bloody April, his nerves only temporarily restored by his tour of home duty. He fussed at being assigned to fly a promising but unfamiliar new biplane designated the S.E.5, even though its 150-horsepower V-8 engine and two machine guns gave him a much better chance against the Albatroses than would his old Nieuport. He persisted in flying lone patrols until he was out of ammunition and dangerously low on fuel—heroic habits in the good days of 1916, but virtual suicide now against the disciplined onslaught of the *Jastas*.

Yet his skill had not deserted him, and he had downed 15 more planes through May 7, when he took off with a patrol in an S.E.5 and ran into a *Jasta 11* flight led by Lothar von Richthofen. While Ball was engaged in one part of the twisting dogfight that followed, Lothar focused on another. His opponent was flying a Sopwith triplane, another of the improved designs that were being supplied to the harried British that spring; Lothar and the Sopwith separated after an inconclusive

Heraldic shields of aviation

Wings were the proud symbol of identification worn by pilots of both the Allies and the Central Powers. Besides the badges for army pilots shown on this page, there were distinctive insignia for naval pilots of each nation and for aerial observers of both services. Some wings, such as the embroidered cloth badges of the United States and Great Britain, were highly stylized. Italy and Austria-Hungary, on the other hand, chose realistic sculptures of eagles, crafted in remarkable detail.

The Central Powers limited their heraldic impulses to badges to be worn on the tunics of their fliers, but most Allied air services extended the practice in colorful profusion to their planes as well *(overleaf)*.

FRANCE

UNITED STATES

GREAT BRITAIN

ITALY

GERMANY

OTTOMAN EMPIRE

AUSTRIA-HUNGARY

Emblems to rally round

Squadron insignia, though they defied the principles of camouflage, helped Allied pilots develop a sense of allegiance to their units. The British were content with simple geometric patterns, but the other Allied air services tacitly encouraged originality in the designs of these emblems, which each unit emblazoned on the sides of its planes.

A selection from the hundreds of different insignia that resulted is displayed here. They range from classic to comic; some of them, such as the French stork and the American hat-in-the-ring, became better known than the official designations of the units they represented.

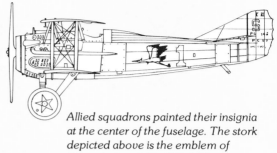

Allied squadrons painted their insignia at the center of the fuselage. The stork depicted above is the emblem of France's Escadrille SPA.167.

FRENCH ESCADRILLES

C.18   AR.35   N.89   N.124 (Lafayette)

V.B.135   SOP.207   SOP 231   V.R.292

ITALIAN SQUADRONS

83rd   91st   94th

UNITED STATES AERO SQUADRONS

9th

11th

13th

49th

88th

90th

94th

99th

104th

141st

186th

213th

BELGIAN ESCADRILLES

2nd

3rd

7th

duel. Then, according to Lothar's later report, the triplane rushed back at him. But it seems likely that Lothar was mistaken; this latest attack appears to have come from a different aircraft. Some accounts say that it was Ball, flying his S.E.5 biplane, who went hard after an Albatros that broke away from the battle. Ball's target soon crash-landed on the German side—just as Ball himself disappeared into a cloud, oil streaming from his engine.

It was Lothar von Richthofen, his gas tank punctured, who tried an emergency landing close to the lines. His opponent came out of the cloud and then fell to the ground. Lothar, wounded in the hip by ground fire, survived. Albert Ball, untouched by enemy bullets but mortally injured in the crash, was lifted from the wreckage and died in the arms of a French farm girl.

Manfred von Richthofen remained on furlough into June and was away from the front when the British launched a fresh artillery and infantry attack against the Hindenburg Line. Once more, swarms of British planes flew into the teeth of the *Jastas*. This time, through weight of numbers and force of spirit, the Royal Flying Corps won back local control of the air.

The most conspicuous symbol of the indomitable zeal in the RFC was the charming Canadian roughneck Billy Bishop, who had managed to get to the front as a combat pilot despite a checkered training record that had landed him on home defense duty in England.

Bishop knew he was a clumsy flier. But he loved a good scrap, and he kept requesting a transfer to the front, until finally he was sent to France. His performance did not improve, however, and after crash-landing a Nieuport at the feet of some important visitors—including the brigade commander—Bishop learned he would be sent back to England. Undaunted, he went up the next day with a small flight of Nieuports, to be confronted near St. Léger in Belgium by three of the latest model Albatroses. One of them went for Bishop.

The chances were slim of a rookie pilot in a Nieuport surviving a face-off with a new Albatros. But Billy Bishop responded to individual combat with a swift instinct that even the Richthofen brothers could not surpass. "I had a quick impulse," Bishop said, "and flew straight at the attacking machine." He drove the enemy plane into the ground with such a wild, gun-rattling dive that Bishop's own engine sputtered and seemed about to die. He saved himself with a lightning pull-out followed by a masterful landing in the shell-pocked mud, a bare 300 yards from the German line.

Billy Bishop had found his calling. German planes began to fall almost like rain before his guns; by the end of the summer of 1917 he had the astounding total of 47 victories. "I had found the one thing I loved above all others," he recalled. "To me it was not a business or a profession, but just a wonderful game."

Playing the game with a joyous vengeance, Bishop spent Easter

Albert Ball, flying an S.E.5 (center), is shown in fatal pursuit of a German Albatros in this painting of Ball's last flight on May 7, 1917. Already the first triple winner of Britain's Distinguished Service Order, Ball was posthumously awarded the Victoria Cross and France's Légion d'Honneur.

Sunday engaging three planes and a balloon before taking on five German planes in a single-handed attack that left two planes burning on the ground—and left Bishop's squadron mates with the impression that "I was some sort of wild man from the zoo." Soon he was awarded the Military Cross and was granted permission to fly alone if he preferred—which he often did. One day in June he set off at dawn for a solitary raid on a German airfield far behind the lines. There, he reported, he destroyed three enemy planes, one after the other, as they rose to meet him. Although there were no friendly witnesses to confirm the exploit, Bishop received the Victoria Cross.

The British were bolstered by increased deliveries of two new aircraft, the single-seated Sopwith Camel with twin Vickers machine guns and the durable two-place Bristol F.2B. But even these planes and such individual heroics as Billy Bishop's were not enough to hold control of the air for long. On June 14, Manfred von Richthofen returned to the front, much as Oswald Boelcke had the year before, with orders that were part of a new German air strategy. Richthofen's charge was to put together the first *Jagdgeschwader (JG* for short), a mobile fighter group of some 50 planes. The aircraft and pilots of *JG 1,* made up initially of four *Jastas,* including his own, would be housed in tents and portable sheds so they could be shuttled by truck or train to any critical point on the battle line.

To help Richthofen's group, and three subsequent ones like it, prevail against increasing odds, the Germans sent long-range bombers over England, hoping they would create sufficient commotion to draw fighter strength away from the front. On June 13 at high noon, 14 twin-engined Gothas circled unhindered over London, dropping bombs that inflicted nearly 600 casualties. The British government recalled two crack fighter squadrons from France and diverted other planes to bolster the home defense strength. "My reserve is dangerously low," groused Royal Flying Corps Commander Hugh Trenchard at this alarming reduction in his frontline aircraft.

The stage had been set for Richthofen—by now promoted to captain—and he entered with a flourish of four quick victories that took him into July with a total of 56. Richthofen liked to approach his prey from above and the Albatroses in his command could fly very well at 18,000 feet. The new master of *JG 1* flew boldly at the point of a stepped V formation that enabled his fighters to protect one another until they dropped like falcons on unwary Allied planes.

Elaborating on the colorful example of *Jasta 11,* which retained its predominantly red paint jobs, the rest of Richthofen's expanded command began taking on every imaginable hue. One pilot recalled "machines with green wings and yellow noses, silver wings with gold noses, red bodies with green wings, light blue bodies and red wings." British airmen dubbed this aerial display the Flying Circus, both for its kaleidoscopic colors and for its circus-like habit of folding its tents and moving overnight from place to place. Billy Bishop scorned them as the "harlequins of the air," but few other Allied fliers saw anything clownish about the Flying Circus or the deadly way it went about the business of what Richthofen called "diminishing the number of our enemies."

British losses grew so severe that inadequately trained replacements were sent aloft as pilots and gunners to face seasoned German airmen. Among the French the pilot shortage was at least as bad. American Charles Biddle, flying as a volunteer with a French squadron, reported that in July of 1917 he went into the air "without any aerial gunnery training at all. Our first shooting practice was in combat over the lines."

The Germans usually made short work of such neophytes, though a two-seater crew from this battered array of ill-trained Allied aviators very nearly did in Captain von Richthofen. Flying near Ypres on July 6, he watched with amusement as an apparently inexperienced British gunner opened fire on his plane from 300 yards away. Richthofen let him use up ammunition: "One does not score at that distance," he remembered thinking. Just then a chance shot plowed a three-inch furrow across his scalp, splintering the bone and knocking him nearly unconscious. In shock, he nursed his plane to the ground, passed out and awoke in the hospital at Courtrai. "My thick Richthofen head proved itself," he remarked.

By late July the baron was back in action. In August he scored two more victories, and another pair in early September for a total of 61. He

A ground crewman (left) helps a German aviator adjust his electrically heated flight suit, whose exposed wires attest to its primitive design. Developed for high altitude reconnaissance flights, the suit was controlled by a rheostat in the cockpit.

was unable to have a 61st cup made, however; the jeweler in Berlin had run out of silver. But by now Richthofen was finding less pleasure in the hunt. His head hurt, and after each patrol he felt "completely exhausted." Periodically, doctors dug out more bone fragments from beneath the scar on his head. Over the next six months he was to shoot down only two enemy aircraft.

In September, the Allies and Germans traded the lives of two more heroes. Georges Guynemer's 54 victories ranked him first among Allied airmen and second in the War only to Richthofen. Earlier in the year, Guynemer had jauntily waved safe passage home to a young German antagonist, Ernst Udet, when Udet's guns jammed in the middle of a fight. Now Guynemer's nerves were frayed and his health was poor. Obsessed more than ever with "bringing down his Boche," he had been ranging deeper and deeper into enemy territory, flying hour after hour and pushing himself to the breaking point. The style of his attacks, formerly so calculated and precise, had deteriorated; he had become foolhardy and was given to fits of anger and depression. To a civilian friend he revealed a presentiment of doom. Like Ball, he said, "I know I shall end by staying there"—at the front. "I have been waiting for this since my very first flight."

On the morning of September 11, Guynemer's wait came to an end. Over Poelcapelle he attacked a two-seater, missed on the first pass, and then vanished into a cloud from which no one saw him emerge.

France would not accept Guynemer's death, even though word filtered across the trenches that two German soldiers had found his body and had buried it hastily in a mud grave that became hopelessly chewed up by artillery bombardments. Soon thereafter the German Foreign Office publicly announced that Guynemer had been shot down.

Still, France was loath to admit that its Winged Sword had been shattered. In a memorial service—not an official funeral—at St.-Pol-sur-Mer, a battalion drew up bearing the wind-snapped flags of 20 regiments. A band played the "Marseillaise," a reprise of the anthem the soldiers had sung on the day Guynemer had risen so wondrously from the wreckage of his crash-landing at Verdun. Then General Paul-François Anthoine, his voice rising and falling in the gusty sea breeze, declared that "no trace could be found" of the missing flier; it was "as if the heavens, jealous of their hero, had not consented to return to earth what seems to belong to it by right." An admiring journalist put it more simply: "He flew so high he could not come down again."

No such romantic mystery attended the fall on September 23 of Lieutenant Werner Voss, whose own victory total had reached 48. Voss perished in full view of seven British S.E.5a pilots whom he had chosen to battle alone in his new Fokker Dr.I triplane. The Dr.I was perhaps the most maneuverable machine at the front, and during a 10-minute fight—from which one of the British fliers said the German had ample opportunity to escape—Voss slashed and wheeled like a barracuda.

To prevent oxygen starvation at high altitudes, some German airmen carried canisters of liquid oxygen like the one above. The oxygen flowed into a rubber bladder and the pilot (below) wore a nose clip and breathed through a long tube.

His aerobatics were "wonderful to behold," according to another of the Englishmen. "The pilot seemed to be firing at all of us simultaneously." But the odds were too great, even for Werner Voss; at length Lieutenant A. P. F. Rhys Davids raked the German with a fatal burst.

Rhys Davids, told the next morning that his victim was the highly esteemed Voss, expressed regret at having killed such a worthy opponent. But the French ace René Fonck was not troubled by such lofty misgivings the following month when he brought down Kurt Wissemann, the pilot whom the Germans officially credited with shooting down Georges Guynemer. Fonck told a journalist that by killing "the murderer of my good friend" he had become "the tool of retribution."

In fact, Guynemer and Fonck had not been close friends. But Fonck, who was a magnificent aviator and a deadly marksman, was seldom at a loss for words to describe his exploits. Even his closest friend in the Storks conceded that he was frequently tactless, and when Fonck first became an ace in 1917, he described the achievement as "my new-found glory." His seventh kill convinced him that he "had become a virtuoso." Eventually he would claim "120 victories of which I, myself, am certain."

The most exasperating thing about René Fonck was that much of what he said about himself was true, or close to it. He became France's successor to Guynemer—and more. His confirmed victory total (as opposed to his unsubstantiated claim) eventually reached 75, highest among all Allied fliers. He flew with unquestionable virtuosity. Once in a 10-second sequence of three quick machine-gun bursts, Fonck shot down three German planes, and twice in the course of the War he brought down six enemy planes in a single day. But for all his fighting skills, Fonck was too abrasive to take Guynemer's place as a popular hero—and he never came close to matching Richthofen's talents as an aerial tactician.

Manfred von Richthofen was raising German fighter tactics to a deadly science. By early 1918 he had traded his Albatros for a Fokker Dr.I, whose excellent rate of climb suited his insistence on keeping above the enemy and whose quickness to the touch met his demand for precise maneuver. But he displayed little interest in his own victory total, which stood more than a dozen ahead of his nearest competitor; instead he spent much of his energy training new pilots.

As a teacher, Richthofen had no patience with show-offs who sought to confound the enemy with dazzling aerobatics. "Flying tricks while fighting," he insisted, was "just reckless and useless," since it put the stunter in a position where he could not shoot. Formation flying was another of Richthofen's favorite topics: "Surprises can be avoided only when flying in close order," he emphasized. "No machine should be allowed either to advance or keep back."

Richthofen may not have realized how much he had begun to sound like Oswald Boelcke. Like his old mentor, he kept hammering at the

Manfred von Richthofen's scarlet Albatros D.III is second in line in this photograph of Jasta 11, taken at Douai in 1917. In April, the Jasta's red-daubed planes scored 83 victories and British fliers labeled the month "Bloody April."

The senior Baron von Richthofen (left) visits his famous son in the German hospital at Courtrai in July 1917. Wounded in the head, Manfred returned to duty after a few weeks but he suffered recurring headaches and bouts of depression.

basics that he believed would save German lives. Time and again he cited the overriding importance of fighting spirit, the ability to act calmly in the face of chilling danger. "The decisive factor in victory," he said, "is simple personal courage."

One of Richthofen's most courageous pilots, Ernst Udet, was a latecomer to the Flying Circus. In an early dogfight, Udet had frozen at his gun and had flown home without having fired a shot. But he had overcome his fear and had blossomed into an ace with 19 confirmed victories when Richthofen recruited him from another *Jasta.* On his first mission with *Jasta 11,* in March 1918, Udet flew behind Richthofen, keenly aware that the leader always kept a close eye on his pilots—especially the new ones. "He judges a man by what he accomplishes," Udet said later of Richthofen. "He who passes this judgment, he backs all the way. Whoever fails, he drops without batting an eyelash. Whoever shows lukewarm on a sortie has to leave the group—the same day."

Udet was determined to pass muster. When the *Jasta* passed a British two-seater, he broke toward the enemy, curled under him for one lethal burst, and within one minute had returned to the *Jasta.* Richthofen's head turned briefly to Udet and he waved his approval. Then the baron dived at a flight of Sopwith Camels, blew one out of the air, and leveled off just above the ground to strafe a column of Allied troops whose machine guns, in return, punched bullet holes in his wings. "We were flying and firing close behind him," Udet recalled. "The entire *Staffel* was a body subject to his will."

Udet had more than passed muster; his performance had earned him a unit command. When the *Jasta* landed, a smiling Richthofen walked past his newest pilot, then said over his shoulder: "By the way, you can take charge of *Jasta 11,* starting tomorrow."

It was well for Germany that Richthofen had another top-flight *Jasta* leader, and that he himself was back in top form—the Sopwith Camel had been Richthofen's sixth victory since mid-March, giving him a total of 69 kills. But inwardly the baron was far from optimistic about Germany's immediate future. "The battle now taking place on all fronts has become awfully serious," he wrote. "There is nothing left of the 'lively, merry war,' as our deeds were called in the beginning. Now we must fight off despair and arm ourselves so the enemy will not penetrate our country."

On the face of it, such gloom seemed unwarranted during the early months of 1918. The Bolsheviks had taken Russia out of the fighting. The French Army was still recovering from a widespread mutiny that had swept the trenches the previous year. Four hundred thousand British troops had fallen in persistent drives against the Hindenburg Line, and the exhausted survivors were close to the point of refusing further attacks. A last-gasp assault by 380 English tanks had been turned aside by counterthrusts of German infantry; one third of the aircraft flying cover for the tanks had been destroyed by German fighter planes and antiaircraft fire.

Not a single American plane had yet appeared over the Western Front, and United States General John J. Pershing was squabbling with the other Allied commanders over how the relatively few United States Army divisions in Europe should be used. Germany, its western armies reinforced by 42 divisions from the east after Russia signed a separate peace, was preparing its most devastating assault since Verdun. Germany's aim was to drive a wedge between the British and French Armies and force their surrender before American strength could become effective. Ludendorff massed some 70 divisions for an attack against the British right flank south of Arras, supporting his infantry with poison gas, 6,000 cannon and 730 planes. The British had just 579 aircraft with which to face the initial assault; for the first time in the War, Germany would enjoy numerical air superiority over a broad sector of the front. "Our planes," Hoeppner promised Ludendorff, "will guarantee your success."

On the foggy first day of spring, March 21, 1918, the Germans jumped off behind a cloud of poison gas and a violent artillery barrage. The British lines broke, allowing the Germans to advance 14 miles in four days. The French, too, fell back, and German planes stormed above both armies, strafing, bombing, and harassing Allied reinforcements as they moved forward.

Richthofen once more threw himself wholeheartedly into the air battle. His command moved to a new forward base at Léchelle, freshly vacated by the British, and on March 27 the Flying Circus flew 118 sorties, bagging 13 Allied aircraft while suffering no losses of its own. Richthofen himself shot down three enemy planes, raising his score to 73. But Richthofen and many other German fighting men sensed that the attack was their nation's last great gamble. The German artillery bombardment had suffered from a lack of ammunition. Supplies of men and matériel had reached bottom, and at home there was no improvement in the food shortage that had led civilians to speak of 1917 as "the turnip year." If the attack did not succeed, the Germans at last would be fighting on their own hearthstones.

For a time the offensive went as planned, and Richthofen, providing close support from a field at Harbonnières, scored four more kills in the first week of April. Abetted by ground fire, German airmen brought down more than 1,000 British planes during March and April. But Richthofen, once the cheerful huntsman of the air, had become depressed by the whole bloody business. "I am in wretched spirits after every battle," he confessed. "When I set foot on the ground again I go to my quarters and do not want to see anyone or hear anything."

On April 8, *JG 1* was ordered to Cappy, on the Somme, where several days of rain and the resulting lull did nothing to improve Richthofen's mood. Then on April 20 the weather brightened a bit; he took to the air again and shot down his 79th enemy airplane, a Sopwith Camel. The pilot, Major Richard Raymond-Barker, died in the crash. Before heading home Richthofen spotted yet another Sopwith and sent it down with a bullet through the fuel tank. Its pilot, 19-year-old Lieutenant D. G. Lewis, was only slightly injured in his forced landing. He reported that Richthofen "flew down to within 100 feet of the ground and waved" before turning back to his base.

As Richthofen climbed down from the cockpit of his red Fokker, he seemed happy—almost jubilant—for the first time in several months. "Eighty!" he exulted. "That is really a decent number." His fellow pilots heartily agreed; that night they feted their captain and drank to him as "the one-man army, our leader, our teacher, and our comrade, the ace of aces."

The next morning, a Sunday, Germany's Ace of Aces climbed once more into his scarlet triplane. Within moments he was aloft at the head of a six-plane formation, churning over the Somme toward the trenches, searching for prey.

On the Allied side that overcast morning, Captain A. Roy Brown's ulcer was acting up; the 24-year-old Canadian aviator knew that what he needed most was sick leave. Without zest, he took off to lead a five-plane patrol that included an old school friend, Wilfred May, who had not yet experienced aerial combat. Soon enough, the formation ran up against a formidable flight of German aircraft. Roy Brown, by his own admission, quickly gave up hope of surviving the engagement.

As the dogfight raged over the road between Sailly-le-Sec and Le Hamel, May broke off and headed for home, as Brown had instructed him to do if a serious battle began. At that moment, a bright red Fokker triplane hurtled from the swirling mist and maneuvered into firing position behind the withdrawing May. Brown rushed to protect his friend, wheeling his Sopwith Camel around and raking the German triplane with fire from his twin Vickers machine guns. "A full burst ripped into the side of the airplane," Brown recalled. "The pilot turned around and looked back. I saw the glint of his eyes behind the big goggles, then he collapsed in the seat."

The red Fokker flew on in pursuit of May for more than a mile before dropping to a rough landing alongside some trenches manned by Australian troops. By the time the plane came to a stop, its pilot was dead.

Back at his base, Brown was writing his report when the telephone rang. The squadron's engineer answered, then shouted to Brown that he had better get ready to receive a medal. "What for?" asked Brown. "The old man says the red flier was Richthofen," replied the engineer.

Later that day—even as Australian ground troops were claiming that they had shot down the red triplane, thus launching a dispute that never has been settled—Roy Brown made his way quietly to the tent where the body of Captain Manfred von Richthofen lay on a sheet of corrugated iron. "He looked so small to me, so delicate," Brown wrote later. "His cap had been removed. Blond, silk-soft hair, like that of a child, fell from the broad high forehead. His face, particularly peaceful, had an expression of gentleness and goodness, of refinement." Brown turned and walked away. "I did not feel like a victor," he said. ∿

Captain A. Roy Brown of Canada, credited by many with shooting down Richthofen, had 11 victories at the time of the disputed triumph. Shortly afterward he entered a hospital for treatment of ulcers and was invalided to England.

Honors for a fallen foe

A British officer wearing a black arm band led the funeral procession. Behind him marched an honor guard of 13 Australian soldiers, their rifles reversed. In a crude wooden coffin on the back of a British tender, Captain Manfred von Richthofen was carried to a grave in France.

The Allies buried their German nemesis with the honors due his rank and with approbation that was remarkable after almost four acrid years of war. Late in a sunny April afternoon the cortege made its measured way from an Australian airdrome, to which Richthofen's body had been brought the previous day, through the budding countryside to a small cemetery ringed with poplar trees, near the village of Bertangles. The casket was laden with wreaths sent in tribute by nearby Allied squadrons; Allied aviators were his pallbearers.

At the cemetery, an Anglican chaplain conducted the burial service. Three volleys were fired and a bugler played "The Last Post."

Richthofen had fallen 11 days short of his 26th birthday. Seven years after the War, his coffin was disinterred and carried through Germany on a ceremonial train to a hero's burial in Berlin.

At a slow march, British and Australian officers and men escort a truck carrying the body of Manfred von Richthofen along the bank of a canal in northeastern France.

An honor guard drawn from the ranks of No. 3 Squadron, Australian Flying Corps, salutes as a British chaplain, wearing a surplice over his uniform, leads Richthofen's casket through the gates of the cemetery at Bertangles. The pallbearers, like Richthofen, were squadron leaders and held the rank of captain.

French villagers, in the foreground, and some 50 Allied airmen, behind the hedge at rear, stand in respectful silence as the Australian honor guard fires a last salute. On the shaded grave was placed a large wreath, sent from British headquarters and inscribed to Captain von Richthofen, "our gallant and worthy foe."

144

JOIN THE
ARMY AIR SERVICE
BE AN AMERICAN EAGLE !
CONSULT YOUR LOCAL DRAFT BOARD. READ THE ILLUSTRATED
BOOKLET AT ANY RECRUITING OFFICE, OR WRITE TO THE CHIEF
SIGNAL OFFICER OF THE ARMY, WASHINGTON, D.C.

5
A timely spur to victory

The Yanks were coming, in ever-increasing numbers. Since the autumn of 1917, units of the American Expeditionary Force commanded by General John Pershing had been fighting on the Western Front, and on April 14, 1918, a week before the death of Richthofen, a pair of German planes fell to the guns of planes bearing the red, blue and white roundel of the United States. Those two were the first of some 850 planes and balloons that would be shot down by American units before the Armistice in November.

In those final convulsive months the airplane came of age with lusty effectiveness in the furious collisions of men and machines that decided the Great War. By midsummer more than 8,000 military aircraft were in action along the Western Front. Every offensive and counteroffensive was accompanied by massive air battles in which dozens or sometimes scores of German and Allied planes streaked through the sky at speeds of 130 miles per hour and altitudes up to 20,000 feet. Strafing, reconnaissance, artillery spotting and photography played telling roles in each battle, and bombing achieved a scope and potency few men had believed possible only a year before. At midyear Allied bombers destroyed the bridges behind an advancing German army, helping to strangle the last great German offensive. And in September the largest air force ever assembled—1,500 fighters and bombers under an aggressive American officer named William "Billy" Mitchell—lashed out in support of an American ground attack that eliminated a powerful German salient near Verdun.

Great Britain had resolved a lingering problem on April 1, 1918, ending years of fraternal bickering and lack of coordination by combining the Royal Flying Corps and the Royal Naval Air Service into a single Royal Air Force. Major General Hugh Trenchard became the RAF's first chief of staff.

Germany, trying urgently to prepare for the day when the United States would bring the full force of its fresh resources to bear, had set about enlarging its Air Service through what it called the *Amerikaprogramm*. The extraordinary effort was to be completed by March 1918; it called for boosting aircraft production to 2,000 planes a month, finding 24,000 recruits and doubling the output of aviation fuel.

For a time, Germany's Air Service was better manned and better equipped than ever, but eventually the *Amerikaprogramm* fell short; an Allied naval blockade prevented adequate supplies of raw materials

The American eagle is more than a match for the bedraggled war bird of Imperial Germany in this 1918 recruiting poster for the Army Air Service. The United States entered the War with fanfare in April 1917, but a year passed before a United States squadron scored a victory.

from reaching Germany and there was a scarcity of suitable candidates for pilot training. For the first time, the fighting will of Germany's home front began to waver.

The role of the United States in the War can be compared to the role of the airplane itself: It was useful, if seldom predominant, and at certain critical times it made the difference between defeat and victory. By April of 1918 a "bridge of ships" was transporting American soldiers to France at the rate of one hundred to two hundred thousand a month. General Ludendorff, the German Chief of Staff, called the Americans "those grinning cowboys," but the fresh troops of the AEF became the stiffener that kept the worn fabric of the Allied line from tearing under the repeated, increasingly desperate slashes of the German armies. The Americans were inexperienced, but they had come to fight. Their first severe test came early in June at Château-Thierry, where two United States divisions helped the French repulse a German onslaught that once more had reached the River Marne.

American air power was slower to make itself felt. Many survivors of the Lafayette Escadrille and the other American volunteers flying for France put on American uniforms and became instructors, flight leaders and squadron commanders. The United States, in time, would produce a covey of aces, but first it had to assemble an air fleet almost from scratch and train the men to fly it. The process took many months; many of the mistakes that had plagued the original belligerents in 1914 and 1915 were repeated, and the lofty promises and ambitious production goals promulgated when the United States entered the War were based more in enthusiasm than in fact.

In June of 1917 the U.S. War Department put forth a plan to build 22,625 airplanes and twice that many engines in a single year. The chief of the United States Signal Corps, of which the Aviation Section was a small part, appealed to the nation to "put the Yankee punch into the war by building an army of the air, regiments and brigades of winged cavalry on gas-driven flying horses." Congress voted to spend $640 million for military aviation—the largest sum it had *ever* appropriated for a single purpose.

But aviation in the United States was practically a stillborn industry. In the 13 years since Kitty Hawk, the United States had produced no more than 1,000 planes of all kinds. Its military air fleet was a hodgepodge of aircraft, useless for combat and barely acceptable as trainers.

In June the United States Army dispatched to Europe a large delegation headed by Major Raynal Bolling to find out what was needed to get the American air effort moving. Based on the Bolling Commission reports, the United States decided to buy its fighter planes abroad, chiefly Spads and Nieuports from the French, and to concentrate at home on building trainers and reconnaissance planes. Instead of designing new planes, the United States contracted to build American versions of several foreign designs. Chief among them was the de Havilland D.H.4, a

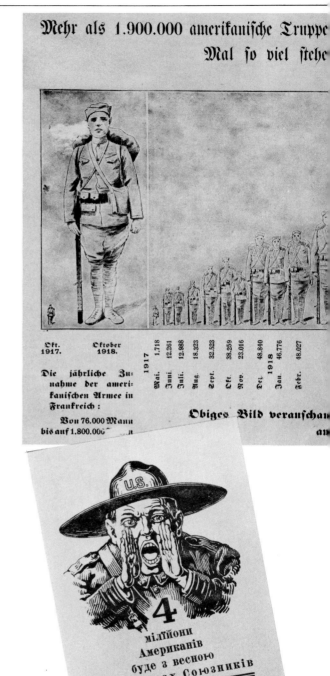

Propaganda leaflets dropped from Allied aircraft in 1918 trumpeted the arrival of masses of American soldiers. The growth of U.S. forces in Europe is illustrated for Germans in the leaflet at top. Above, in a leaflet aimed at Ukrainians fighting for Austria-Hungary, a soldier warns of millions more Americans on the way.

Ogni minuto otto soldati Americani sbarcano in Europa!

In a leaflet dropped over the Italian front, doughboys stride across a clockface with the legend, "Every minute eight American soldiers disembark in Europe."

two-seated reconnaissance bomber with a 400-horsepower American-designed Liberty 12 engine. Eventually 1,213 of these hybrids were built and some 400 of them saw action on the Western Front.

The next step was to find qualified aviators and mechanics. Before the Declaration of War, the Army had barely two dozen combat-ready pilots, plus an additional 113 men in flight training. But there was no shortage of volunteers. Some 38,000 young men, many of them the elite of their generation, sought to enlist in the air arm, attracted, as 1916 Yale graduate Harold Tittmann explained, by the fact that "the opportunities for advancement appeared limitless, it was clean work and had a romantic appeal." Above all, Tittmann concluded, "I would not have the responsibility of leading men to that slaughter which was inevitable in the trenches. In the airplane, you alone profited from your skill or suffered for your mistakes."

American flight training was standardized into three phases: ground, primary and advanced. Ground schools of two to three months' duration were established on eight college campuses—the largest ones at the Universities of Texas and California. Among them they enrolled some 23,000 volunteers, of whom about three fourths went on to primary flight training at military airfields, most of them newly built. There they learned to fly at the dual controls of slow Curtiss JN-4 biplanes called Jennies. The Bolling Mission arranged for American fliers to take their advanced training at facilities in Great Britain, France and Italy where experienced instructors and more sophisticated airplanes were available. The European centers were soon clogged with more Yankee pilots than they could handle, and much of the advanced training program reverted to makeshift camps in the United States. One of the most famous of them, Kelly Field in Texas, consisted of little more than "six canvas hangars, a few shacklike barracks, and a collection of squad tents, in which we were quartered," according to a trainee who reported there in 1917. "Cleared of its sagebrush and cactus," he said, "the landing field was no more than a flat piece of desert."

Eventually this hastily devised system produced 10,000 American aviators; a companion program turned out a like number of aviation mechanics. Harold Tittmann attended ground school at the University of Texas, then reported for primary training to Chanute Field at Rantoul, Illinois. "I never felt so frustrated as I did at Rantoul," Tittmann wrote later in an unpublished memoir. In 10 weeks he managed "barely 25 hours of flying time" in the few available Jennies. Tittmann was certified a reserve military aviator and commissioned a first lieutenant. By November of 1917, he and hundreds of other young aviators were on troopships bound for Europe and final training.

Tittmann reported to Issoudun, 125 miles south of Paris. Issoudun was the largest of 22 centers at which Americans would train in France, but when Tittmann arrived, its collection of eight airfields and attendant buildings were still under construction. "German prisoners of war and laborers from French Indochina worked under the supervision of

A chance to aid the war effort and to wear a snappy uniform attracted thousands of women to the WRAF.

Top-flight help at a cut-rate price

Women contributed substantially to the air-war effort, often in jobs previously reserved for men. In England, women served as auxiliaries and, after April 1, 1918, in the Women's Royal Air Force. Posters like the one at left recruited them for traditional women's work. In practice, however, many women became airplane mechanics and factory workers—though for half the pay men received.

Due in part to the effort of women, aircraft production in Britain rose from 2,000 a year to 2,000 a month. By the War's end, 25,000 women were in the WRAF, but not one flew a military plane.

Four female mechanics overhaul an Avro trainer flown by gunnery students in England.

Seamstresses of the WRAF sew the linen that was used to cover airplane surfaces. Coated with dope, it created a taut, durable surface.

French engineers," he wrote. "The winter was exceptionally cold and the area was one mass of alternately frozen or oozing clay." American doctors decided that the manure piles in the nearby farmyards threatened the health of those on the base. Since prisoners of war were not allowed to work near the French houses, American soldiers got the job of removing the manure. Peasants stood by, Tittmann wrote, wondering "why the presence of their fertilizer, which had been part of their lives as long as they could remember, should suddenly be regarded as something unhealthy."

The Americans, for their part, had to learn the French way of flying. Tittmann and the others had been taught by an instructor in the dual-control Jennies. Now they were introduced to the *rouleur,* a single-seater that was normal in every way except that the wings were too small to lift the plane off the ground. After hours of gunning around the airstrip in a *rouleur* the novices were given an unclipped plane and simply told to fly it. Next the Americans advanced to airborne gunnery drills aboard rehabilitated Nieuports—two of Tittmann's friends lost their lives when the wings of their planes collapsed in mid-flight.

In April of 1918, Tittmann was assigned to Orly Field near Paris, where he discovered in his off-duty hours that the favorite haunt of American aviators was the bar of the Hôtel de Crillon overlooking the Place de la Concorde. There, he reported, the socializing began every evening at 5 p.m. and continued despite the intrusion of German Gotha bombers that attacked the French capital on almost every clear night.

Between soirées at the Crillon, Tittmann's job was to ferry new planes from Paris to the handful of United States squadrons that finally were forming behind the front. Fresh from French factories, the planes were not yet armed. It was a situation that dismayed Major Raoul Lufbery, recently the leading ace of the Lafayette Escadrille, who had just become flight leader of the 94th Aero Squadron. "It's nearly a year since the United States declared war," Lufbery groused. "And what do you suppose the 94th is doing? Waiting for machine guns."

Unwilling to wait on the ground at Villeneuve-les-Vertus, the 94th's temporary home, Lufbery took his eager pilots on patrol in their weaponless planes. The first time he tried this hazardous exercise, he took along the two most promising of his new fliers: a handsome 21-year-old Harvard graduate named Doug Campbell and a tough-talking, long-legged 27-year-old grammar school dropout named Eddie Rickenbacker. Though Lufbery kept his charges from crossing any distance into German-held territory, they found plenty to worry about.

Rickenbacker had an especially rough time. "My Baby Nieuport pitched and rolled violently," he recalled. "I began to experience the first pangs of airsickness. I clenched my teeth and prayed." Suddenly he was startled by an explosion only a few feet behind him. The Germans had baptized him with antiaircraft fire, scaring him so thoroughly that he lost "all thoughts of airsickness." During the remaining two hours of the patrol, Rickenbacker's apprehension gave way to excitement and final-

Eddie Rickenbacker, America's top ace, stands in the cockpit of his French-built Spad 13. A former race-car driver, Rickenbacker adapted quickly to fighter planes and scored 26 victories—20 of them in the last two months of the War.

ly to an almost euphoric cockiness at flying over a real battlefield with Lufbery, the most celebrated aviator in American uniform.

Eddie Rickenbacker had learned most things in life the hard way. Born in Columbus, Ohio, in 1890 to a German immigrant family that had retained the old-country spelling of their name—Rickenbacher—Eddie had battled his way upward, relying on a quick wit and fast reflexes. When he was 13 his father died, and he went to work at a series of factory jobs to help support the family—starting on the night shift at a glassworks. He was hired by a small automobile company that turned out one car a month, and by 16 he had become a crack race-car mechanic. Before he turned 20 he was established as a winning driver in his own right, and the newspapers began calling him the "Wild Teuton." His front-running style soon earned him a world land-speed record of 134 miles per hour and an income of more than $35,000 a year.

On a visit to England in late 1916 he discovered that the "Teuton" publicity and his Germanic name had attracted the attention of Scotland Yard. Ever alert to spies, agents surreptitiously dismantled his shoes and ripped open the linings of his clothes. Once they detained him and ordered him to strip so lemon juice could be applied to his skin in a vain search for secret messages. The experience persuaded Eddie to change the spelling of his name to Rickenbacker—it seemed less German.

Returning home, Rickenbacker tried to persuade the United States Army to form a special fighter squadron made up of racing drivers, on the plausible theory that quick-acting men accustomed to high speeds in tight places would make excellent fliers. The Army said no, adding that Rickenbacker himself was too old and had too little formal education to qualify. Once the United States declared war, however, the celebrated auto racer had no trouble enlisting and getting himself assigned as a driver to the American general staff in France. Soon word spread that he was General Pershing's personal chauffeur. "It's a good story," Rickenbacker noted, and he let it stand. He did, in fact, drive for Colonel Billy Mitchell and it was with Mitchell's blessing that Rickenbacker soon transferred to flight school at Tours. There he earned his wings in just 17 days, "not because I was supersmart," he conceded, "but because I had had some experience in speed, motors, and knew mechanics."

Rickenbacker soon earned a reputation as a man who "merely had to listen to an engine to tell what was wrong with it." He was sent to Issoudun as an engineering officer to organize the school's repair shops and motor pool. His mother had cautioned him in a letter to "fly slow and stay close to the ground," and for a time it appeared that staying close to the ground would be his fate. He also gained a reputation as a crude roughneck among his colleagues, most of whom had grown up on the other side of the tracks. "Rickenbacker was about the most unpopular man alive in those early days," said Reed Chambers, a future squadron mate. "He was big, older, tough as nails. His race track vernacular, his profane vocabulary, didn't set right with the cream of American colleges."

The potent planes that Britain built

After a slow start, Great Britain steadily gained momentum in the race to design and produce combat aircraft. The B.E.2 was an early mainstay among RFC reconnaissance planes but even in late versions *(bottom left)* it was slow and unmaneuverable, and thus an inviting target.

By mid-1917, British aircraft had improved enormously. The de Havilland D.H.4 *(lower right)* was chosen by the United States for manufacture under license. And Britain's most advanced fighters, the Royal Aircraft Factory's S.E.5a *(right)* and the Sopwith F.1 "Camel" *(below),* provided a potent one-two punch. British ace James McCudden praised the S.E.5a as "far and away superior" to enemy planes, and the Camels logged more kills than any other plane in the War.

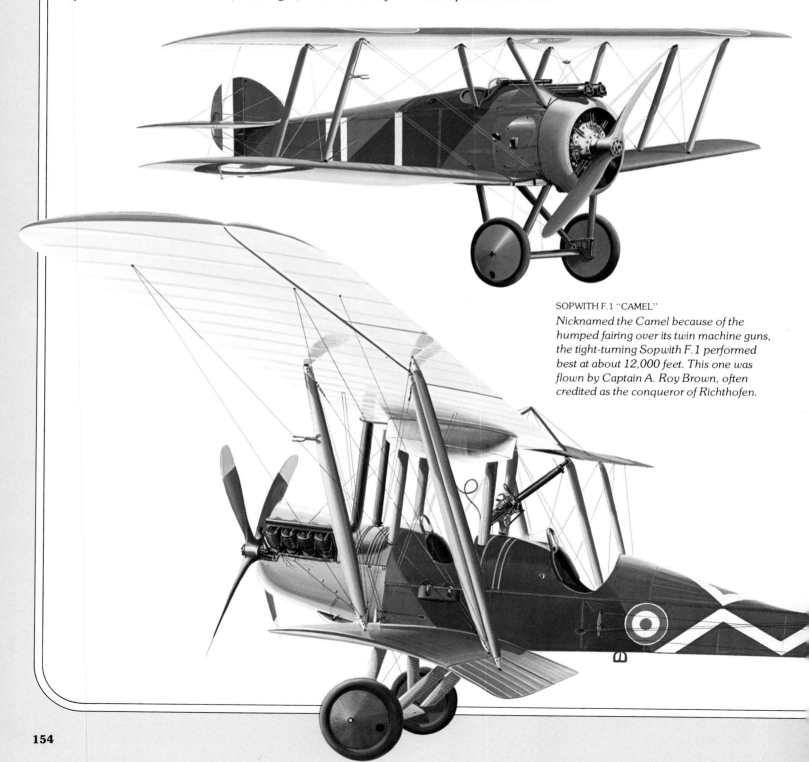

SOPWITH F.1 "CAMEL"
Nicknamed the Camel because of the humped fairing over its twin machine guns, the tight-turning Sopwith F.1 performed best at about 12,000 feet. This one was flown by Captain A. Roy Brown, often credited as the conqueror of Richthofen.

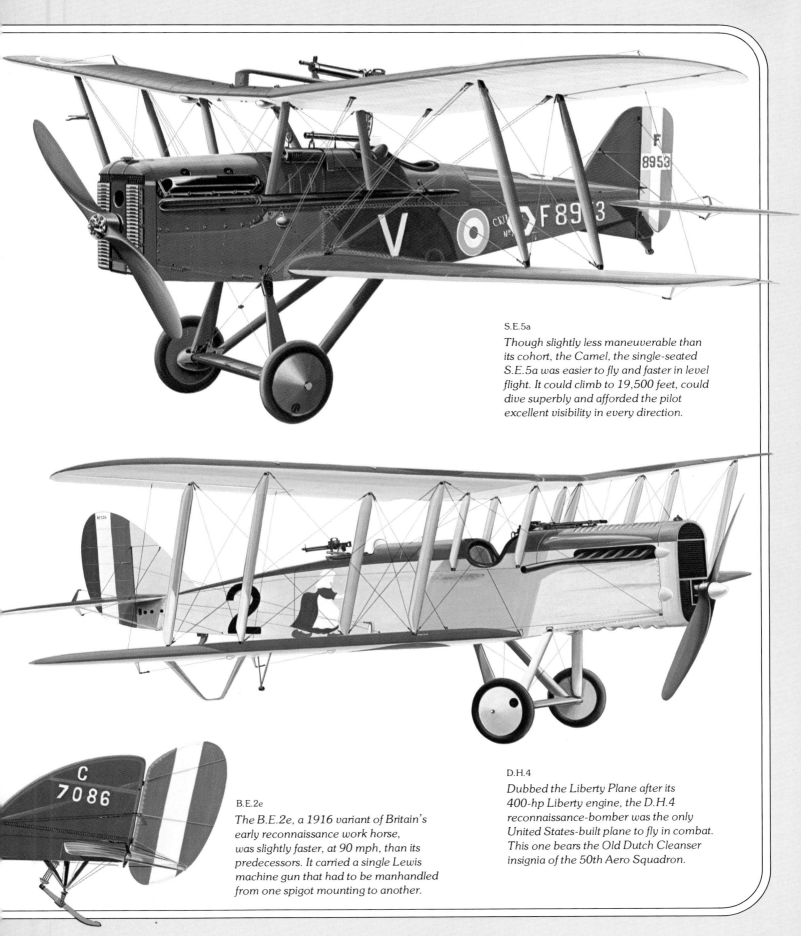

S.E.5a

Though slightly less maneuverable than its cohort, the Camel, the single-seated S.E.5a was easier to fly and faster in level flight. It could climb to 19,500 feet, could dive superbly and afforded the pilot excellent visibility in every direction.

B.E.2e

The B.E.2e, a 1916 variant of Britain's early reconnaissance work horse, was slightly faster, at 90 mph, than its predecessors. It carried a single Lewis machine gun that had to be manhandled from one spigot mounting to another.

D.H.4

Dubbed the Liberty Plane after its 400-hp Liberty engine, the D.H.4 reconnaissance-bomber was the only United States-built plane to fly in combat. This one bears the Old Dutch Cleanser insignia of the 50th Aero Squadron.

None of this fazed Rickenbacker, who began slipping off in Nieuports at odd hours to expand the basic flying skills he had acquired so quickly. In January of 1918 he talked the commanding officer at Issoudun, Major Carl "Tooey" Spaatz, into sending him to gunnery school at Cazaux, from which he transferred in March to the 94th Aero Squadron. Rickenbacker's ground-bound days were over, but his standing with his fellow aviators did not immediately improve. "When Rick came over," said Chambers, "the rest of the pilots immediately ostracized him. He threw his weight around the wrong way." But, Chambers added, "he learned a lot after he joined the squadron."

Once more, the lessons came hard. The 94th moved to an airdrome at Toul and finally received its machine guns, but Rickenbacker failed to distinguish himself on the squadron's first armed patrol. Fog forced the flight commander to turn back, but Rickenbacker—followed by Reed Chambers—kept on hunting for Germans. They became lost in the fog and Rickenbacker barely managed to find his way back to the field—without Chambers. As he climbed down from his plane, prepared to be chewed out by the flight leader, an operations officer interrupted with a shout: "Quick! Two Boche airplanes. Send an alert!"

Doug Campbell and another American named Alan Winslow took off. Three minutes later a private ran past Rickenbacker yelling that a German airplane "has just fallen in flames on our field!" Moments afterward another German machine hit the ground not a quarter of a mile away. Accounts differ as to which of the two Yanks, Campbell or Winslow, had registered the first official American victory of the War. But there was no question who had set it up: The German pilots were both captured; they had tailed Rickenbacker and Chambers into a fog bank and emerged, to their chagrin, over the American airfield.

The double success for the 94th on its first day of armed operations was a great boost for the Americans. Cablegrams and telephone calls of congratulation poured in. The wreckage of the German planes was exhibited in the Toul town square, much to the joy of the inhabitants, who milled around the American aviators, kissing them, toasting them and shouting *"Vivent les Américains!"* Reed Chambers, needless to say, found his way out of the fog in time to join the celebration.

Eddie Rickenbacker, a loner who rarely raised a social glass with the boys, became more determined than ever to get some Germans of his own. For two weeks he patrolled in search of a victory, surviving two close brushes with death. The first came from a case of mistaken identity; a French Spad dived at him repeatedly until Rickenbacker banked his own machine to give the Frenchman a clear view of the American insignia painted on his wings. The second close call occurred when Rickenbacker flew through a cluster of antiaircraft bursts to attack a German plane that seemed strangely unconcerned by his approach. At the critical instant Rickenbacker glanced over his shoulder—to see three Albatroses diving at the foolish American who had gone after the decoy. He darted into a large cloud and circled inside it until it seemed

An RAF pilot of an S.E.5a displays a sign in mid-1918 announcing that his squadron has downed 39 planes in 14 days.

A photograph found in many a German pilot's scrapbook depicted a skull gripping a 50-mark note in its teeth—a grisly commentary on the "danger money" German airmen received for flight duty.

Above an Iron Cross, a propeller inscribed to "Our Brave Heroes" marks the graves of two German fliers who were shot down in Belgium and buried with other war dead in a cemetery in Flanders.

safe to run for home. Rickenbacker got away; although his victory total remained at zero his education, at least, was proceeding rapidly.

On April 29, he went out on patrol with James Norman Hall (who would later co-author the seafaring classic, *Mutiny on the Bounty*). Hall had served in the Lafayette Escadrille and, like Lufbery, had come to the 94th squadron as a flight leader. On this day the two Americans spotted a German Pfalz fighter in time to climb above it and attack out of the sun. Hall dived at the unsuspecting Pfalz, while Rickenbacker stayed high and worked eastward to cut off the German's retreat.

Dodging away from Hall, the Pfalz turned directly into the path of Rickenbacker's guns. He opened fire and the Pfalz heeled over and crashed near a copse of trees inside the German lines. Hall celebrated his partner's first kill with a frenzy of aerobatics, despite a furious barrage sent up by German antiaircraft batteries that had seen the fight.

The 94th, still eager and enthusiastic about the War, made much of such things as first victories. The pilots had established an unofficial but rigid hierarchy within the squadron, complete with made-up titles. Lowest in the pecking order were newly arrived replacements, called Vultures since they had no planes and, essentially, were waiting for someone to become a casualty. Once a Vulture got his own plane he became a Buzzard, and was required to mark his promotion by downing a liter of champagne in the mess while singing the squadron's fight song.

By scoring his first kill, Buzzard Rickenbacker became a Goofer, above which stood only the ruling class of Guimpers—the flight leaders and squadron commander. Remote and tough though Rickenbacker was, he admitted feeling deeply pleased at the warmth of congratulations on his victory. In that sense, at least, he had been accepted.

Through the month of May, Rickenbacker developed a deliberate, lethal style of combat and added new victories to his record. One morning before daylight, he flew 20 miles behind the lines before he circled back toward the German airdrome at Thiaucourt. Above the enemy field he throttled down his engine and went into an almost silent glide to increase the element of surprise. He saw three Albatroses taking off, trailed them unnoticed toward the front, then pounced on the rearmost one. "As the distance closed to 50 yards I saw my tracer bullets piercing the back of the pilot's seat," he wrote. "The scared Boche had made the mistake of trying to outdive me instead of outmaneuvering me. He paid for his blunder with his life." The action almost cost Rickenbacker his own life. As he pulled out of his attack, he heard a crash "that sounded like the crack of doom." The top right wing of his Nieuport had collapsed and he watched its canvas covering blow away. Just a few days earlier the same thing had happened to James Norman Hall, who had crashed and was taken prisoner. Rickenbacker was more fortunate. Calling on all his instincts and experience as a racing driver, he brought the plane level and nursed it back to Toul, where he "grazed the top of Old 94th's hangar" and pancaked onto the field.

By May 30th, flying high and picking his targets with care, Ricken-

For the greater glory of Empire

Of the thousands of airmen who served under the Union Jack in World War I, only 19 earned Great Britain's highest military decoration, the Victoria Cross—sometimes for a single act, sometimes for repeated acts of valor. All 19 are shown here, with the dates in which they won the award. Four received it posthumously; five others did not survive the War.

The Victoria Cross winners came from all parts of the Empire. Among them were three Canadians, a South African, an Australian and an Irishman. They ranged widely in age—from 19 to 32—and in social background. Some of them were well-to-do and college educated; others were men of little means and scant schooling. What they had in common, one commanding officer wrote, was "the guts of a lion."

WILLIAM RHODES-MOORHOUSE in May 1915 posthumously became the first airman to win the Victoria Cross.

R. A. J. WARNEFORD, June 1915; killed that month

JOHN LIDDELL, Aug. 1915; died later that month

LANOE HAWKER, Aug. 1915; killed Nov. 1916

GILBERT INSALL, Dec. 1915

RICHARD BELL-DAVIES, Dec. 1915

LIONEL REES, Aug. 1916

WILLIAM LEEFE ROBINSON, Sept. 1916

THOMAS MOTTERSHEAD, Feb. 1917 (posthumous)

FRANK McNAMARA, June 1917

ALBERT BALL, June 1917 (posthumous)

WILLIAM BISHOP, Aug. 1917

JAMES McCUDDEN, March 1918; killed July 1918

ALAN McLEOD, May 1918; died Nov. 1918

ALAN JERRARD, May 1918

FERDINAND WEST, Nov. 1918

WILLIAM G. BARKER, Nov. 1918

ANDREW BEAUCHAMP PROCTOR, Nov. 1918

EDWARD MANNOCK, July 1919 (posthumous)

backer had scored his fifth victory. But the latest victim fell so far behind the German lines that confirmation would be slow in coming—if it came at all. The next day Doug Campbell achieved his fifth kill—shooting down a Rumpler two-seater whose observer, out of ammunition, had stood defiantly in the cockpit with arms folded as Campbell's bullets drove the plane to earth. The Rumpler fell in Allied territory and the victory was quickly confirmed; Doug Campbell officially became the first ace among the newly arrived Americans.

Two weeks later confirmation of Rickenbacker's fifth victory came from the French Eighth Army. The United States—and the 94th—now had a pair of aces. But the squadron with the sportily belligerent hat-in-the-ring insignia was in no mood to celebrate these successes; its best pilot was dead. Raoul Lufbery had built a total of 17 victories, including those collected while he was with the Lafayette Escadrille. One day he went up alone near the field at Toul to confront an Albatros on which an inexperienced American pilot had futilely used up all his ammunition at long range. After one pass, Lufbery pulled away, apparently to clear a jammed gun. When he went back to the attack, his plane was seen to falter, then smoke, and finally burst into flames as it slipped out of control toward the little village of Maron. While still several hundred feet above the ground, Lufbery either jumped or fell from the cockpit, landing on a picket fence that marked a flower garden. "Just think," wrote an angry Billy Mitchell, who had witnessed the beginning of the action. "If he had had a parachute he could easily have been saved." But even the loss of its foremost pilot was not enough to impel the United States government to issue the still-unperfected life-saving devices.

As bombing raids proliferated, so did the ground defenses against them. At left, below, an Italian artilleryman listens through a portable device called a sheerophone. It consisted basically of a large, flat resonator; sound waves emitted by approaching aircraft engines caused the sheerophone to vibrate. On a snow-covered road (below) French civil defenders scan the sky with mobile searchlights.

Lufbery's death came at a time of change and increasing responsibility for American aviators in France. In late May the Aviation Section was removed from the Signal Corps and became a separate entity as the United States Air Service, under Brigadier General Mason Patrick. The 94th was united with the 95th, 27th and 194th squadrons into the 1st Pursuit Group. Three observation squadrons were operating regularly, and a bomber squadron, the 96th, was forming. Plans were afoot to concentrate all these units as the 1st Brigade air service under Colonel Mitchell and move it to the critical Château-Thierry sector.

However, the loss of key men and a subsequent slump in morale plagued the still very young United States Air Service. Within days of becoming an ace, Doug Campbell was wounded so severely he did not recover until the very end of the War. Rickenbacker, who had replaced James Norman Hall as leader of the 94th's first flight, began to feel debilitating waves of pain from a mastoid infection that would put him out of combat for several weeks.

Late in June the Americans moved as planned to the Marne—70 planes of the pursuit group one day, observation squadrons close behind. "The best groups in German aviation were in front of us," wrote Colonel Mitchell; they were the "red-nosed pursuit group" until recently commanded by Richthofen and two other *Jagdstaffeln* that Mitchell considered equally good. Mitchell's French counterpart urged that American planes be used in defensive patrols along the front. Mitchell protested this discredited tactic, but he went along with it until he realized that it was "merely suicide" for patrols of five or six planes to stand up to German formations of 20 to 30. "In a few days we lost many good

Warned of impending attack, a British antiaircraft team rushes to its guns near Armentières in 1916. The guns fired 13-pound shells that could bring down a plane flying as high as 19,000 feet.

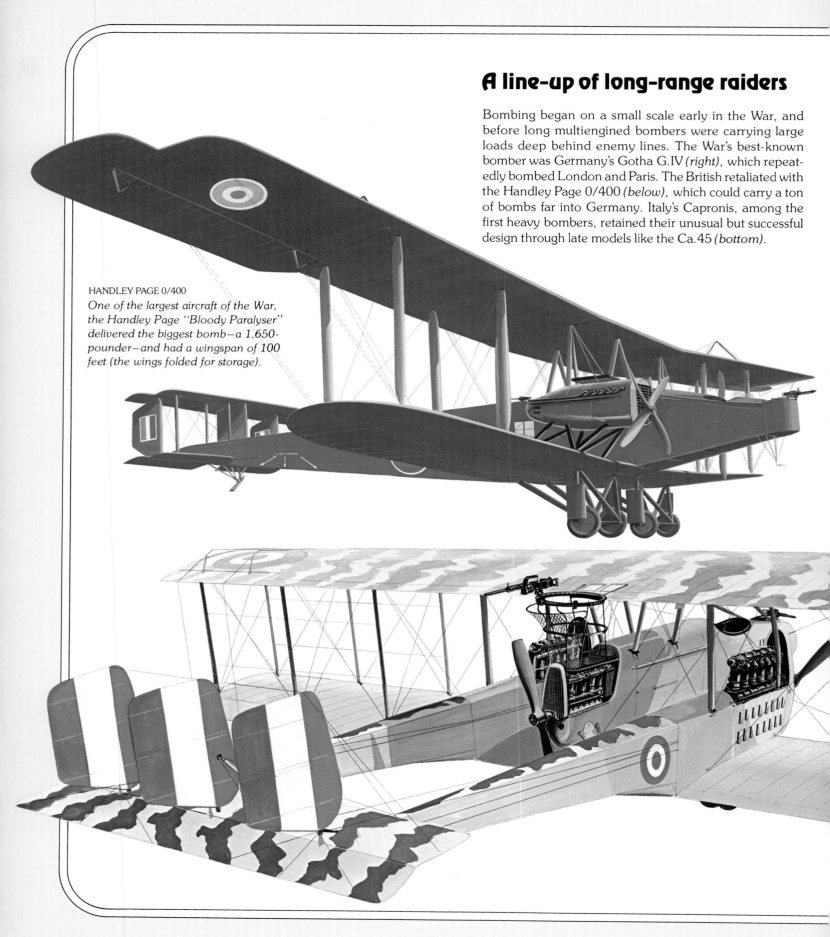

A line-up of long-range raiders

Bombing began on a small scale early in the War, and before long multiengined bombers were carrying large loads deep behind enemy lines. The War's best-known bomber was Germany's Gotha G.IV *(right)*, which repeatedly bombed London and Paris. The British retaliated with the Handley Page 0/400 *(below)*, which could carry a ton of bombs far into Germany. Italy's Capronis, among the first heavy bombers, retained their unusual but successful design through late models like the Ca.45 *(bottom)*.

HANDLEY PAGE 0/400
One of the largest aircraft of the War, the Handley Page "Bloody Paralyser" delivered the biggest bomb—a 1,650-pounder—and had a wingspan of 100 feet (the wings folded for storage).

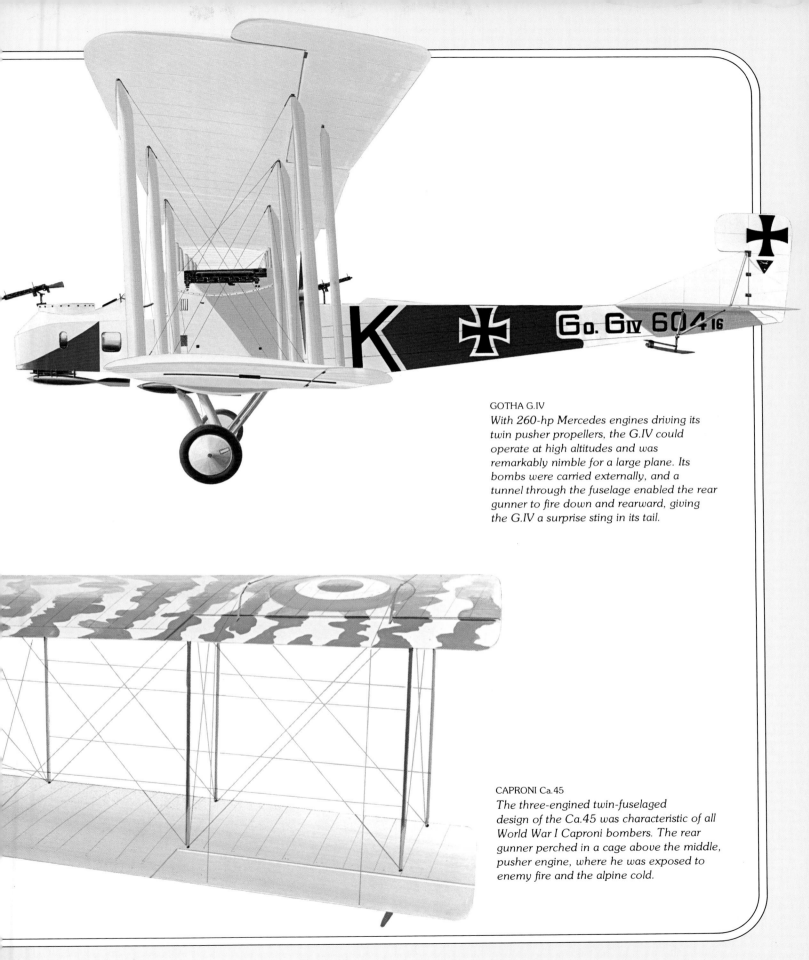

GOTHA G.IV

With 260-hp Mercedes engines driving its twin pusher propellers, the G.IV could operate at high altitudes and was remarkably nimble for a large plane. Its bombs were carried externally, and a tunnel through the fuselage enabled the rear gunner to fire down and rearward, giving the G.IV a surprise sting in its tail.

CAPRONI Ca.45

The three-engined twin-fuselaged design of the Ca.45 was characteristic of all World War I Caproni bombers. The rear gunner perched in a cage above the middle, pusher engine, where he was exposed to enemy fire and the alpine cold.

men," Mitchell wrote. One casualty was Harold Tittmann, who had joined the 94th a few weeks before. He lost a leg after a crash landing that hurled him 30 feet from his plane. Another was Quentin Roosevelt, son of the former President, who lost his life when he became separated from his flight and was attacked by seven red-splashed Fokkers.

The Americans pressed their reconnaissance work, by night now as well as by day. But they were limited in numbers as well as experience, and through the summer of 1918 the air conflict remained primarily a war of attrition between the long-standing foes. In June the Germans, using Tony Fokker's latest and best plane, the superbly maneuverable D.VII, shot down 487 Allied aircraft while losing 150 of their own. British and French factories were able to more than make up for the lost machines, but it was difficult to compensate for the disproportionately high numbers of Allied lives that were lost.

By June, with the single exception of René Fonck, every surviving Allied pilot with 40 victories or more flew for the RAF. Among them, the most successful were Billy Bishop and the telephone worker who in 1914 had been interned by the Turks, Edward "Mick" Mannock. After nine months away from the front on a recruiting tour of Canada and as a gunnery instructor in England, Bishop had returned to France in May to take command of the 85th fighter squadron. He had barely settled in when he received a message that Canada did not want to risk its foremost air hero after all; he would have to come home for good.

Bishop set out to make his last fling at combat something special. Between May 27 and June 18, in his S.E.5a he shot down 20 German aircraft, raising his total to 67. On June 19, he knocked five more Germans out of the sky. In less than 37 hours of flying time he had brought down 25 planes. Then, as ordered, Billy Bishop went home.

Of all the young men who flew over the Western Front, Mick Mannock may have been the most complicated. His soldier father had deserted Mannock's Irish-born mother and four young children when Mick was in his early teens; he was already blind in his left eye from a steadily worsening astigmatism. From boyhood, a dislike of social rank and dissatisfaction with traditional British politics had smoldered within him. He grew up to be a radical socialist, and in the British air service he showed almost as much antagonism toward his officers as he did toward the Germans. When General Trenchard visited the airfield to which Mannock was assigned in France in 1917, Mannock wrote in his diary: "Talked bilge. Don't like him. Too schoolmastery."

Still, Mannock was capable of intense loyalty and affection, and these feelings were now directed toward his fellow fliers. Sometimes he played his violin for them, turning his face shyly to the wall. At other times he would joyfully scuffle with his mates in "mess rags"—indoor rugby scrums in which a pillow was used in lieu of a ball. But each time one of his friends fell in flames or was reported missing, a wrenching sorrow would come over him. He would retire to his quarters, sobbing, with his head in his hands, repeating the man's name over and over.

The masterful eye of photographer Edward Steichen, shown in his flying gear (above), is evident in the photograph at right of the remains of the village of Vaux. Steichen was Chief of the Photographic Section of the United States Air Service in 1918 when he recorded this desolation caused by air-directed artillery fire.

Mannock himself had an ineradicable fear of fire, and never stopped carrying aloft the service revolver with which he vowed "to finish myself as soon as I see the first sight of flames." When Mannock first reached the front his fear almost prevented him from flying at all. He was overcome by waves of nausea before a patrol and on one occasion, when his gun jammed and the engine temporarily failed, he landed "with my knees shaking and my nerves all torn to bits."

His first victory was over a balloon. Then despite hours of gunnery practice, his second kill eluded him. Some of his squadron mates intimated that, in the words of the squadron commander, "he was suffering from cold feet." Called to account for his timidity, Mannock admitted: "I've been very frightened." But, he vowed, "Having conquered myself, I'll now conquer the Hun." Satisfied, his commander gave up any ideas about having Mannock transferred out of the air service.

By sheer force of will, Mannock began to turn himself into an efficient killer. The long hours of gunnery practice had given him a shooting skill that more than compensated for his blind eye. Driven, perhaps, by a desire to prove he had conquered his fear, he now shoved his plane's

Pictures too good to be true

From the moment the spectacular photographs on these pages were first published in 1932, they set off a controversy as spirited as the dogfights they purport to show.

Ever since, historians, photographic experts and former World War I pilots—some of whom conceded that aerial combat did look like this—have argued over whether the photographs were faked. They had been made public by Mrs. Gladys Cockburn-Lange, the widow of a British flier. She refused to identify the photographer or anyone else who could authenticate the pictures. An anonymous diary, allegedly written by the photographer and describing how the pictures were taken, only fueled the dispute.

Critics have maintained that the photographs are too sharply focused to have been shot, as the diary claimed, by a camera mounted on a twisting, vibrating airplane. Others point out that contemporary cameras lacked the depth of field to capture clearly in a single frame such scenes as the 14 planes doing battle at far right, below.

In 1979 experts in the Time-Life Photo Lab studied prints from the collection. Their conclusion: The photographs are not genuine.

nose tight against real targets. Of one victory he noted, with a conscious callousness, "I was only 10 yards away from him—on top so I couldn't miss. A beautifully colored insect he was—red, blue, green and yellow. I let him have 60 rounds, so there wasn't much left of him."

As though to exorcise his own fears, Mannock gustily referred to planes he set afire as "flamerinoes." After visiting one wreck he said of the pilot, "There were three neat little bullet holes right here"—pointing to his temple.

Mannock's success won him a promotion to flight commander in March of 1918, and the responsibility made him protective, almost fatherly, toward the young pilots in his charge. As Boelcke and Richthofen had done, he carefully took newcomers aloft on their first patrols, and he lectured them on the tactics of survival and success. "Sight your own guns," he advised. "The armorer hasn't got to do the fighting." Good flying alone never beat an enemy, he warned. "You must learn to shoot." Mannock went so far as to set up kills for some of his more uncertain youngsters, going ahead rather like a professional hunter to drive the prey into the neophyte's guns. For no one knew better than Mick Mannock how frightened a young flier could be.

Mannock's compassion did not extend to his country's enemies. "There was absolutely no chivalry with him and the only good Hun was a dead one," said one of his squadron mates. When the news came of Manfred von Richthofen's death and the usual toasts were offered for the dead rival, Mannock walked out of the mess in disgust. One day when Mannock shot down four Germans, he bounced into the mess shouting, "Flamerinoes—four! Sizzle-sizzle wonk!"

But his successes—and his fears—were taking their toll. On home leave in June of 1918 with 59 official victories to his credit, Mannock, who had just turned 31, disturbed his friends with his haggard appearance, his unrelieved tenseness and his incessant talk of the War's horrors. He had a recurrent dream of falling in a burning plane and cried frequently. Despite his unstable condition he returned in July as commanding officer of Squadron 85. As his score mounted into the sixties, he received the shattering news that James McCudden, one of his former instructors and one of Britain's leading aces, had been killed.

Somehow Mannock kept going, leading his squadron effectively and raising his own total to 72 kills by July 22. "I've caught up with Bishop's score," he told a friend, only a little cheered by the achievement.

"They'll have the red carpet out for you after the war, Mick," said the friend. Mannock replied: "There won't be any 'after the war' for me."

Several days later, Mannock rose at dawn to take up a young pilot named Inglis. He lit a pipe, played "Londonderry Air" on a scratchy gramophone, and when Inglis arrived, walked to his plane. As he climbed in, he cocked his ear to the early-morning trill of a songbird. "He's like me, full of the joys of life," Mannock smiled wryly, and took off. Heading east he spotted a two-seated L.V.G. over German territory. Mannock waggled his wings and Inglis followed him into a steep

Hermann Göring, shown with his medals and other memorabilia, took command of the Flying Circus two months after Richthofen's death and was personally credited with 22 kills. In 1935 he became chief of a resurgent German Luftwaffe.

dive. Mannock's guns raked the L.V.G., which burst into flames; it was his 73rd victory, making him top British ace. But Mannock had broken one of his own rules by "following the Hun too low" to the ground. The Germans sent up a storm of ground fire. Suddenly, as Inglis watched, an orange flame appeared on the right side of Mannock's fuselage.

No one will ever know whether Mick Mannock used the gun he carried for the purpose to shoot himself at that instant, for the Allies never located the wreckage of his plane. But his left wing suddenly swung over and the plane hit the ground, bursting into a consuming flame. Inglis, his own plane hit, managed a crash-landing just inside British lines. A rescue crew found him curled up in the cockpit, crying.

In mid-July the weary German army attacked once more at the Marne. There could be no further attempt if this one did not succeed. It did not. French and American divisions held their ground, then counterattacked, forcing the Germans back across the river. On August 8, the Allies at last took the initiative, launching a great offensive at Amiens, on the Somme. Before sundown, the Germans had been thrown back eight miles; General Ludendorff called it a black day in German military history. Yet it was anything but that for the pilots of the German *Jagdgeschwader* who fought, as they would to the very last day, like men who had no intention of losing the War.

On the first day of the Amiens offensive, the Germans shot down 62 Allied planes; by the fourth day the toll had reached 144, while the Germans had lost only 30 of their own. The Fokker D.VII that the Germans were flying possessed extraordinary climbing ability. When attacking from below, its resistance to stalling gave Allied fliers the exaggerated impression that a D.VII pilot could bring his plane to a standstill in the air with the nose straight up and spray his victim with lead.

Despite the loss of Richthofen and other aces—and the difficulty of finding and training capable replacements—Germany's best pilots had developed the confidence that comes with experience and success. In *Jagdgeschwader 1,* Ernst Udet was vying with his comrade Erich Loewenhardt for the leadership in victories among all German airmen. Udet had 51 and Loewenhardt 53 on the August day when Loewenhardt was killed in a mid-air collision.

Command of the Flying Circus had been inherited in July by a gruff martinet named Hermann Göring, an arthritic former infantryman who did not believe in the independence of action that Richthofen had granted his flight leaders. Yet Göring proved himself an effective leader in difficult times. Along with the other group commanders, he kept up the fighting spirit of his pilots while Germany's land forces fell back in the face of a sustained Allied assault along an ever-widening front.

Patrolling over the battlefield, Ernst Udet reported he could "see our men fleeing from their positions, dragging their machine guns along." Still, the German pilots, now usually outnumbered at least two to one, refused to concede air space to the enemy. By late summer they were rationed to 40 gallons of gasoline a day per plane and were running short of ammunition. Udet recalled that if an Allied plane crashed near a German airfield "we stripped it bare because we had long since run out of such fine instruments, shining with nickel and brass." The Flying Circus was ordered north to the Somme, and the pilots had to land on the way to beg fuel from a commandant who had little enough for his own machines. While they haggled, a British machine strafed the sitting Fokkers. Furious, Udet took off, climbed straight at the British pilot and shot him down with a burst of 10 rounds. Then he glided back with a dead stick, out of gas.

In mid-September the American First Army, more than half a million strong, set out to eliminate the long-held German salient at St.-Mihiel, on the southeast flank of Verdun. A mighty force of Allied planes would coordinate its attacks with the army according to a broad strategical plan. The instigator of the idea was Colonel Billy Mitchell, who now had direct command of 49 squadrons, about half of them manned by American pilots, half by French. Additionally, he had been given temporary control of 40 French squadrons and the cooperation of nine British squadrons from a new air group called the Independent Force, RAF. In all, Mitchell held the reins to some 1,500 aircraft, the greatest concentration of air power, he wrote, that the world had ever seen.

The battle began on September 12 with the traditional artillery barrage. But this time 500 fighters and two-seaters also swept over the German positions, strafing and bombing. Simultaneously, two other fleets of 500 aircraft each hit the bases of the salient in alternating waves, blasting the German rear into smoking ruins. An estimated 295 German planes counterattacked, but they could not cope with the Allied armada. Mitchell wrote proudly that on the first day "every objective had been accomplished." His friend Lieutenant Colonel George Patton "rode into St.-Mihiel on the back of one of his tanks, way ahead of any other ground troops in the vicinity." Eddie Rickenbacker, healthy again and flying one of the Spad 13s with which the 94th squadron had been reequipped, had the same impression: "The whole country was swarming with retreating Huns," he said. "Horses plunged and broke. Guns, stores and ammunition were being hauled away."

The salient evaporated, with more than 15,000 Germans surrendering. Rickenbacker scored his sixth and seventh victories, both against Fokkers. Two weeks later he was made commanding officer of the 94th.

At this late hour in the War, the once eager and ambitious Hat-in-the-Ring Squadron desperately needed a strong leader. Despite its part in the St.-Mihiel victory, the morale of the 94th had never really recovered from the poundings of May and June. Only Rickenbacker, Reed Chambers and one other pilot remained from the original group that had formed in the spring.

Rickenbacker's first act was typically American. He called together his pilots for an old-fashioned pep rally. The 94th had lost its primacy among the 12 American pursuit squadrons now at the front, he remind-

Second Lieutenant Frank Luke Jr., American nemesis of German observation balloons, relaxes against the wing of his Spad 13 shortly before his death on September 29, 1918. On five occasions in the preceding 18 days he brought his plane back so badly damaged that each time he had to be given a new one.

General Billy Mitchell (center), a vocal American exponent of strategic bombing, contended that his wartime superiors ran the United States Air Service "with just as much knowledge about it as a hog has about skating." He is flanked here by two experienced air officers, United States Colonel Thomas Milling (left) and France's Major Paul Armengaud.

ed them, and he expected them to get it back. The meeting had just the effect on the 94th that Rickenbacker intended. "He made it back into a team," said Chambers. Next, Rickenbacker talked with the mechanics, those much-ignored men upon whom every pilot's life depended. They knew that at heart he was one of them, able, as one man said, to "get more revs and performance out of an engine than anyone else in the squadron." Clearly, Rickenbacker had matured. "When he stopped trying to win the war all by himself," said Chambers, "he developed into the most natural leader I ever saw."

Rickenbacker next tried to ensure the revival of the 94th by recruiting to it the leading American flier in France. But events intervened. Frank Luke of the 27th squadron had scored 14 victories, 11 of them against German artillery-spotting balloons. Some pilots preferred to avoid balloons, with their defending clusters of antiaircraft guns and rockets. Not Frank Luke. A roughneck copper miner from Phoenix, Arizona, according to Rickenbacker, he attacked "like a whirlwind with absolute cockiness but with never a thought for his own safety." In one five-day period in September of 1918, he sent eight balloons down in flames. On one evening, under the cover of his wingman and best friend, Joseph Wehner, Luke put on a special show for Rickenbacker, Mitchell and 1st Pursuit commander Harold Hartney. Luke pointed out two balloons on the darkening horizon. Then he took off, set the balloons afire within four minutes of each other—as he predicted he would do—and returned to the field laughing.

On the day in mid-September when he shot down two more balloons and three German planes, Luke came home without his partner. He landed asking a question whose answer he already knew: "Has Wehner come back yet?"

Luke did not recover from the loss of his friend. He raised his total kills to 17, but between forays he brooded. Twice he went AWOL to spend the night with friends at a neighboring French airdrome. When he returned, his commanding officer grounded him indefinitely. Luke defied the order by taking off in someone else's Spad, bent on the destruction of more Germans. At a small forward field he stopped to refuel, then headed over the lines, trailed by an order for his arrest.

At sunset a note with a streamer attached arched down onto United States balloon headquarters at Souilly: Look out for three enemy balloons, signed, Luke. While the Americans watched, Luke raced from Dun-sur-Meuse to Brière Farm to Milly, setting off a great blossom of flame at each place. This time it was Frank Luke who did not come back. Wounded while shooting down the second and third balloons, he pressed on to strafe German troops in the streets of a hamlet called Murvaux before setting down his damaged plane. Enemy troops surrounded him. But Luke refused to surrender. He drew his .45-caliber revolver and blazed away until a German rifle bullet brought him down.

On September 26, 1918, the Allies launched the offensive that ended the War. American divisions drove into the Argonne Forest at heavy

A curious tale of captivity

On a September morning in 1918, Lieutenant Guy Brown Wiser of the United States 20th Aero Squadron took off from a French airfield in his D.H.4 to bomb the rail yards at Dun-sur-Meuse. Within hours, Wiser and his observer had been forced down in a dogfight and were taken prisoner.

But, perhaps because he was an aviator, and perhaps because his German captors sensed that the War was nearly over, Wiser's incarceration was more a confused lark than the nightmare experienced by many prisoners of war. One generous German sergeant even gave him a sketch pad and watercolors; Wiser used them to create a cartoon record of his imprisonment, published here for the first time. The paintings and an accompanying diary, said Wiser wryly, are a "modest record of the entertainment accorded us while guests of the German government."

In the two months before his release, Wiser was shuttled in custody from one place to another: private homes, a bug-infested hotel, formidable Karlsruhe prison and finally the stables of a 12th Century Bavarian castle. Along the way he encountered the characters who became the subjects of his cartoons. They ranged from a French baritone, whose off-key singing made nightmares of inmate talent nights, to a fearsome woman barber who wielded scissors and razor "as if her previous training had been on sheep."

While Wiser painted, his fellow prisoners played cards or checkers and haggled over extra cigarettes and razor blades. When a German photographer paid a visit, the prisoners hammed it up for the camera. They then bought prints to send their families, wrote Wiser, "to show the folks back home that we are happy and in good shape."

En route to a new prison, Wiser (facing backward), a fellow captive and three guards ride informally through a battered town.

"Red Evans needs a haircut," wrote Wiser. He got one from a woman barber who worked with "the subtlety of a fullback."

At the pest-ridden Hôtel d'Angleterre, Wiser noted, "it does not take long to realize we are not alone in the room."

While the prisoners play cards, a "pleasant and friendly" German guard (at left) kibitzes between swigs of beer.

At Karlsruhe prison, two inmates mug for a photographer who, Wiser noted, did a "land office business" with the prisoners.

A French prisoner entertains on talent night. "Unless you understand French," complained Wiser, "it's murder."

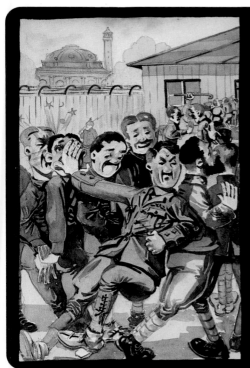

Cigarette lines became shoving contests, wrote Wiser, "when a man gets one pack, then tries to weasel back in."

"Nobody has anything but praise for the American Red Cross," said Wiser. Above, inmates get a supply of Red Cross food.

Self-appointed POW cooks squabble over a menu. "When one insists on beans," sighed Wiser, "the other wants rice."

cost. Aggressive American patrols flew low over the enemy lines, forcing the Germans to fight, and claiming 100 enemy planes and 21 balloons in five days. Billy Mitchell used the 800 planes in his command to bomb concentration points where the enemy was forming to counterattack.

Within a week of taking over command, Eddie Rickenbacker led the 94th back to first place among American squadrons, shooting down three planes himself. He seemed to be everywhere. Over the final weeks of the conflict, reported Reed Chambers, "he drove himself to exhaustion. He'd fly the required patrol. Then he and I would come back to the field, have a cup of coffee, get into our second ships and go hunting by ourselves. Rick always patrolled at just enough rpm's to prevent stalling. He saved the ship for the moment he needed it. When he fought, however, he called for maximum performance and drove the plane until it nearly fell apart. Most of the pilots he killed never knew what hit them. Out of the sun, a quick burst and gone. That was Rickenbacker."

Such tactics brought Rickenbacker's victory total to 24 as October waned. On the ground, meanwhile, the Hindenburg Line collapsed and Allied forces rolled through open country toward the German border. On October 30, Eddie Rickenbacker scored his last two victories, the final one a balloon that gave him 26—highest among all American pilots. The next day he took off for the lines carrying 100 bundled newspapers to drop to the advancing doughboys. When the papers fluttered to earth, the Yanks cheered the news that Turkey had surrendered. Austria would follow on November 3.

After four years of near-stalemate, the end came swiftly. Mutiny broke out in the German High Seas Fleet at Kiel. A Communist-led revolt erupted in Munich. The Kaiser abdicated and a German armistice commission was dispatched to France.

Still the proud men of the *Jagdgeschwader* would not concede. Almost out of gas, out of bullets, out of everything but an unshaken sense of duty, the aviators of the Flying Circus continued to rise each day against the oncoming Allies. By concentrating their forces over a small sector of the front, they were able to achieve, in the words of a contemporary British history, "a strictly local superiority."

On November 10, they bowed to the inevitable. Informed that an armistice would go into effect the next day, each German pilot prepared his own plane for a final flight. It had been agreed that 1,700 specified fighters and bombers would be turned over to the Allies. The rest were free to fly home.

At 94th squadron headquarters, near Rembercourt, Rickenbacker got the word by telephone. "Peace has been declared!" shouted the caller. The cease-fire would begin at 11 a.m. the next day. Momentarily, there was silence. Then, outside, an antiaircraft battery went off in celebration. Immediately, machine guns, rifles, Very pistols, .45s, captured Lugers, horns and sirens let go, interspersed with wild shouts and roars of laughter. Gasoline drums were overturned on the airfield and

As trophies of war, remnants of German aircraft are displayed in the Place de la Concorde in Paris a few days after the Armistice. Germany surrendered 1,700 fighters and bombers to the Allies.

set ablaze; pilots joined hands to dance in manic joy around the fires, while star shells, parachute flares, tracers and rockets lit the sky above. Rickenbacker was seen grappling happily in the mud with one of the squadron's mechanics.

Up and down the battle line the survivors of the Great War lay down their arms in joy and sorrow, and in a shared relief. Casualties in the air had been insignificant, given the awful magnitude of the conflict. Some 9,378 British fliers and 8,212 Germans were dead or missing. French casualties cannot be established; French records for much of 1918 have been lost. The lesser nations had lost lesser numbers. The Americans, arriving so late in the War, had 237 airmen killed in battle; nearly four times as many died of disease and other causes. The airmen's accomplishments, besides the popular immortality accorded a handful of them, were twofold: They had made the airplane, so recently a sporting toy, a powerful machine of war. And they had demonstrated its promise as a machine of immeasurable usefulness in time of peace.

In the years after the Great War, its veterans scoffed at being called knights, though they remembered with enthusiasm the details of every duel. ''I knew I had to kill or be killed,'' said one, speaking for many. ''I didn't enjoy killing. What I enjoyed was the contest.'' 〰

Forgotten battles over a hostile desert

Compared to the mighty conflict in Europe, England's war with Turkey in the Near East was considered a sideshow by some, yet its outcome determined the course of events in that region for decades. A heavy share of credit for the eventual British victory there belongs to an aggressive air unit called the Palestine Brigade. T. E. Lawrence, Britain's legendary liaison to its Arab allies, wrote that in 1918 it was the brigade that "converted the Turkish retreat into rout."

The battleground was "a wilderness of deepcut gorges and barren hills," where aerial photography and reconnais-

sance became vital to the British campaign. Airmen repeatedly headed out over the uncharted wasteland to bomb and scout the Turkish Army. But a downed pilot was in triple jeopardy: Unless rescued swiftly he would be captured by the Turks or killed by hostile Arabs or—the constant peril of the desert—simply die of thirst.

It was a grueling, dramatic but little-known war. In 1919 Stuart Reid, a British artist and flight commander stationed in Egypt, was commissioned to preserve its unique quality. The paintings on these and the following pages are his.

Helpless beside his overturned Nieuport Scout, British Captain Alan Bott is in danger of having his throat cut by Bedouins intent on looting the wreckage. The Arabs fled at the approach of Turkish troops (left), who took Bott prisoner. He eventually escaped.

Turkish soldiers trapped on the heights of the Wadi el Far'a can find no shelter from bombing and strafing by British S.E.5a and Bristol F.2B aircraft in September 1918. The air attack turned the retreat of the Turkish Seventh Army into a massacre.

The desert itself is the enemy in this painting. Lieutenant S. G. Ridley and his mechanic, J. A. Garside, had made a forced landing on June 16, 1916, east of Aswan, Egypt. When found by a search party four days later, their water was gone and both men were dead.

181

Jubilant Arab horsemen celebrate the arrival of a Handley Page at Umm as Surab in 1918. It had brought fuel and spare parts for British planes assigned to Emir Faisal's headquarters. It later was sent to bomb Der'a, a Turkish stronghold.

Although severely injured, Lieutenant Frank McNamara gets airborne in a damaged B.E.2c as Captain D. W. Rutherford scrambles into the observer's seat. Rutherford had made a forced landing in the plane and McNamara, coming to his aid, had overturned his own plane—which he set afire as Turkish cavalry closed in. The rescue earned McNamara the Victoria Cross.

Leading aces by nation

The personal nature of air combat in World War I enabled each nation to maintain a record of the successes of its individual aviators. Ground rules were established for confirming each victory—victory being defined as the shooting or forcing down of an enemy plane, balloon or airship regardless of whether the opposing pilot was killed or survived. Though many victories were never confirmed, literally thousands of airmen were credited with at least one victory. Those with 17 or more are listed here.

AUSTRIA-HUNGARY
40 G. Brumowski
32 J. Arigi
30 F. Linke-Crawford
29 B. Fiala
19 J. Kiss

BELGIUM
37 W. Coppens

FRANCE
75 R. Fonck
54 G. Guynemer
45 C. Nungesser
41 G. Madon
35 M. Boyau
34 M. Coiffard
28 J.-P. L. Bourjade
27 A. Pinsard
23 R. Dorme
23 G. Guérin
23 C. M. Haegelen
22 P. Marinovitch
21 A. Heurtaux
20 A. Deullin
19 H. de Slade
19 J. Ehrlich
18 B. de Romanet

GERMANY
80 M. von Richthofen
62 E. Udet
53 E. Loewenhardt
48 W. Voss
45 F. Rumey
44 R. Berthold
43 P. Bäumer
41 J. Jacobs
41 B. Loerzer
40 O. Boelcke
40 F. Büchner
40 L. von Richthofen
39 H. Gontermann
39 K. Menckhoff
36 M. Müller
35 J. Buckler
35 G. Dörr
35 E. R. von Schleich
34 J. Veltjens
33 H. Bongartz
33 O. Koennecke
33 K. Wolff
32 T. Osterkamp
32 E. Thuy
31 P. Billik
31 K. Bolle
31 G. Sachsenberg
30 K. Allmenröder
30 K. Degelow
30 H. Kroll
30 J. Mai
30 U. Neckel
30 K. Schaefer
29 H. Frommerz
28 W. Blume
28 W. von Bülow
28 F. von Röth
27 F. Bernert
27 O. Fruhner
27 H. Kirschstein
27 K. Thom
27 A. von Tutschek
27 K. Wüsthoff
26 H. Auffahrt
26 O. von Boenigk
26 E. Dostler
26 A. Laumann
25 O. von Beaulieu-Marconnay
25 R. von Greim
25 G. von Hantelmann
25 M. Näther
25 F. Pütter
24 E. Böhme
23 H. Becker
23 G. Meyer
22 H. Göring
22 H. Klein
22 H. Pippart
22 W. Preuss
22 K. Schlegel
22 R. Windisch
21 H. Adam
21 F. Christiansen
21 F. Friedrichs
21 F. Höln
20 F. Altemeier
20 H. Bethge
20 R. von Eschwege
20 W. Goettsch
20 F. Noltenius
20 W. Reinhard
19 G. Fieseler
19 W. Frankl
19 O. Kissenberth
19 O. Schmidt
18 H. Baldamus
18 F. Hemer
18 O. Hennrich
18 K. Wintgens
17 W. Böning
17 E. Hess
17 F. Ray
17 H. Rolfes
17 J. Schwendemann

GREAT BRITAIN
73 E. Mannock
72 W. A. Bishop
60 R. Collishaw
57 J. T. B. McCudden
54 A. W. Beauchamp-Proctor
54 D. R. MacLaren
53 W. G. Barker
47 R. A. Little
46 P. F. Fullard
46 G. E. H. McElroy
44 A. Ball
44 J. Gilmore
41 T. F. Hazell
40 J. I. T. Jones
39 W. G. Claxton
39 R. S. Dallas
37 F. R. McCall
35 H. W. Woollett
34 F. G. Quigley
32 G. H. Bowman
31 A. D. Carter
31 J. L. M. White
30 M. B. Frew
30 S. M. Kinkead
30 A. E. McKeever
29 A. H. Cobby
29 W. L. Jordon
27 J. E. Gurdon
27 R. T. C. Hoidge
27 H. G. E. Luchford
27 G. J. C. Maxwell
26 W. C. Campbell
26 W. E. Staton
25 K. L. Caldwell
25 R. J. O. Compston
25 J. Leacroft
25 R. A. Mayberry
24 J. O. Andrews
24 W. E. Shields
23 J. S. T. Fall
23 A. Hepburn
23 D. Latimer
23 E. J. K. McLoughry
23 A. P. F. Rhys Davids
23 S. W. Rosevear
23 H. A. Whistler
22 C. D. Booker
22 W. J. C. K. Cochrane-Patrick
19 W. Frankl
22 R. King
22 McK. Thomson
22 C. J. Venter
21 P. J. Clayson
21 R. P. Minifie
21 G. E. Thompson
20 D. J. Bell
20 T. S. Harrison
20 W. L. Harrison
20 E. C. Johnston
20 C. F. King
20 I. D. R. McDonald
20 C. M. MacEwen
20 G. W. Murlis-Green
20 K. R. Park
20 D. A. Stewart
19 W. Beaver
19 H. B. Bell-Irving
19 C. E. Howell
19 L. F. Jenkins
19 H. W. L. Saunders
19 A. M. Wilkinson
18 L. M. Barlow
18 C. F. Collett
18 A. K. Cowper
18 F. R. Cubbon
18 E. Dickson
18 A. J. Enstone
18 E. V. Reid
18 F. A. Thayre
18 J. L. Trollope
18 W. B. Wood
17 W. M. Alexander
17 J. H. Burden
17 G. E. Gibbons
17 M. A. Newnham
17 E. Swale

ITALY
34 F. Baracca
26 S. Scaroni
24 P. R. Piccio
21 F. T. Baracchini
20 F. R. di Calabria
17 M. Cerutti
17 F. Ranza

RUSSIA
17 A. A. Kazakov

UNITED STATES
26 E. Rickenbacker
22 W. Lambert
20 F. Gillette
20 J. Malone
18 F. Hale
18 A. Iaccaci
18 F. Luke Jr.
17 R. Lufbery

Acknowledgments

The index for this book was prepared by Gale Partoyan. The editors also thank John Batchelor, artist (pages 64-65, 94-95, 120-121, 154-155, 162-163), Frank Wootton, artist (endpaper and cover detail, regular edition), and Frank J. and Clare M. Ford, cartographers (pages 22 and 87). For their valuable help with the preparation of this volume, the editors wish to thank: **In Belgium:** Anvers—Baron Willy Coppens de Houthulst; Brussels—Gustave Abeels, Historian; Daniel Brackx; Jean Lorette, Chief Curator, Army Museum; Commander Philippe Van Der Stichelen, Belgian Air Force; Mechelen—Lieutenant Colonel Terlinden. **In Canada:** Ottawa—A. A. Azar, Fred Halley, H. A. Halliday, Curator of Art, Richard K. Mallott, Curator of Collections, Canadian War Museum; Ginette Chatel, Public Archives; A. J. Short, Assistant Curator, National Museum of Science and Technology. **In France:** Blérancourt—Reynold Arnould, Chief Curator, Musée National de la Coopération Franco-Américaine; Chamalières—Louis Chartoire, Association des As; Chatou—Donald C. Bartlett; Foix—Pierre Farré; Paris—Maurice Bellonte; François Blech; Cécile Coutin, Curator, Musée des Deux Guerres Mondiales; Charles Juroe; Jean-Claude Lemaire, Fondation du Memorial Escadrille Lafayette; André Bénard, Odile Benoist, Elizabeth Caquot, Lucette Charpentier, Alain Degardin, Georges Delaleau, Gilbert Deloizy, Général Paul Dompnier, Deputy Director, Yvan Kayser, Général Lissarague, Director, Stéphane Nicolaou, Colonel Jean-Baptiste Reveilhac, Curator, Musée de l'Air; Colonel Marcel Dugué McCarthy, Consultant, Colonel Jean Martel, former Curator, Lieutenant-Colonel Marc Neuville, Curator, Colonel Jacques Weimar, Consultant, Colonel Paul Willing, Curator, Musée de l'Armée; Edmond Petit, Curator, Musée Air-France; Mahaut Perthuis de Laillevault; Hélène Rabourdin, Les Vieilles Tiges; Christiane Roger, Société Française de Photographie; Denise Rotival; Maurice E. H. Rotival; Ville d'Avray—Adrien Dagnas; Vincennes—Général Charles Christienne, Director, Patrick Facon, Guy Lechoix, Simone Pesquies-Courbier, Capitaine Madeleine Peyruseigt, Monique Pointurier, S.H.A.A. **In Great Britain:** Harpenden—Alex Imrie; Gloucestershire—Derek G. Arthurs; London—D. M. Condell, J. C. Darracott, Art Department, P. J. Thwaites, Documents Department, and Department of Photographs, Imperial War Museum; A. C. Harold, Research Assistant, D. I. Roberts, Research Assistant, Alison Uppard, Royal Air Force Museum; Norwich—Chaz Bowyer. **In Italy:** Lugo—Guido Baracca; Milan—Rinaldo d'Ami; Maurizio Pagliano, Ali Italiane; Sandro Taragni; Rome—Captain Giovanni Angelini, Ufficio Storico, Captain Giancarlo Fortuna, Ufficio Propaganda, General Giuseppe Pesce, Inspector of the Air Force, Stato Maggiore Aeronautica; Countess Maria Fede Caproni, Museo Aeronautico Caproni di Taliedo; General Mario Tirelli, Director, Museo del Genio. **In the United States:** California—George H. Cooke, Aero Historians of World War I; Charles Palm, Hoover Institution, Stanford University; LeRoy Prinz; Guy Brown Wiser; Colorado—Donald J. Barrett, USAF Academy; James J. Parks, M.D.; Connecticut—V. Allen Hower; Washington D.C.—William Heimdahl, Archivist, Lawrence J. Paszek, Senior Editor, Office of Air Force History; Jerry Kearns, Library of Congress; William Leary, National Archives and Record Service; Dr. Joseph Mehl, Army Center of Military History; Craddock R. Goins, Museum of History and Technology, Dominick A. Pisano, Catherine D. Scott, C. Glenn Sweeting, National Air and Space Museum; Edgar A. Wischnowski; Hawaii—Hilbert L. Bair; Illinois—Robert N. Church; Massachusetts—Charles Woolley; New Jersey—Peter M. Grosz; Walter Musciano; New York—Gerard H. Hughes; James H. C. Palen Jr., Old Rhinebeck Aerodrome; Allen Sanford, Pathé News; New York City—Hilary Knight; Grace Mayer, Museum of Modern Art; Neal O'Connor; Alan Praulx, King Features Syndicate; Ohio—Richard E. Baughman, Royal Frey, Charles Worman, Vivian White, Kathy Cassity, Pete Turner, Joe Skinner, Air Force Museum, Wright-Patterson Air Force Base; A. E. Ferko; Virginia—Dana Bell, USAF Photo Depository; Eric Ludvigsen, *Army* magazine; Wisconsin—Ira Milton Jones, Overseas Flyers of World War I; Steve St. Martin. **In West Germany:** Babenhausen—Heinz Nowarra; Berlin (West)—Dr. Roland Klemig, Heidi Klein, Bildarchiv Preussischer Kulturbesitz; Axel Schulz, Ullstein Bilderdienst; Erlangen—General Karl Bodenschatz; Koblenz—Dr. Matthias Haupt, Bundesarchiv; Munich—Joseph Pöllitsch; Bruno Schmäling; Rastatt—Ulrich Schiers, Henning Volle, Wehrgeschichtliches Museum; Rösrath Hoffnungsthal—Janusz Piekalkiewicz; Stuttgart—Werner Haupt, Bibliothek für Zeitgeschichte; Uetersen—Rudolf Hannemann; Wittmund—Peter Nolde.
The editors also wish to thank Wibo van de Linde, Amsterdam; Pavle Svabic, Belgrade; Carol Pine, Minneapolis, Minnesota; Felix Rosenthal, Moscow; David Good, New Haven, Connecticut; Carlton Proctor, Pensacola, Florida; Beth Cocanougher, Scottsdale Arizona; Peter Allen, Sydney; Ron Graeff, Syracuse, New York. Particularly useful sources of information and quotations were *The Eagle of Lille* by Franz Immelmann, John Hamilton Ltd. Publishers, 1959; *The Great Air War* by Aaron Norman, The Macmillan Co., 1968; *The Red Baron* by Manfred Freiherr von Richthofen, Doubleday & Co., Inc., 1969; *Knight of Germany* by Johannes Werner, Arno Press, 1972.

Bibliography

Books
American Heritage, *History of World War I.* Simon and Schuster, 1964.
Angelucci, Enzo, *World Aircraft, Origins—World War I.* Rand McNally, 1975.
Apostolo, Giorgio, *Color Profiles of World War I Combat Planes.* Crescent Books, 1974.
Baldwin, Hanson W., *World War I, an Outline History.* Harper & Row, 1962.
Bishop, William A., *Winged Warfare.* Ace Books, 1967.
Bordeaux, Henry, *Georges Guynemer, Knight of the Air.* Arno Press, 1972.
Bowyer, Chaz, *Airmen of World War I.* London: Arms and Armour Press, 1975.
Bowyer, Chaz, *Albert Ball, VC.* London: William Kimber, 1977.
Bowyer, Chaz, *For Valour, the Air VCs.* London: William Kimber, 1978.
Boyle, Andrew, *Trenchard.* London: Collins, 1962.
Chapman, John J., *Victor Chapman's Letters from France.* Macmillan, 1917.
Clark, Alan, *Aces High.* G. P. Putnam's, 1973.
Cole, Christopher, *McCudden V.C.* London: William Kimber, 1967.
Cuneo, John R., *Winged Mars,* Vols. 1 and 2. Military Service Publishing Company, 1942.
Douglas, Sholto, *Years of Combat.* London: Collins, 1963.
Drew, George, *Canada's Fighting Airmen.* Toronto: Maclean Publishing Company, 1930.
Elliott, Stuart E., *Wooden Crates & Gallant Pilots.* Dorrance, 1974.
Flammer, Philip M., *Primus Inter Pares: A History of the Lafayette Escadrille.* Dissertation, 1963.
Fonck, René, *Ace of Aces.* Doubleday, 1967.
Funderburk, Thomas R., *The Fighters: the Men and Machines of the First Air War.* Grosset & Dunlap, 1965.
Garros, Roland, *Memoires.* Paris: Hachette, 1966.
Goldberg, Alfred, ed., *A History of the United States Air Force, 1907-1957.* Arno Press, 1972.
Gorrell, Edgar S., *The Measure of America's World War Aeronautical Effort.* Norwich University, 1940.
Gray, Peter, and Owen Thetford, *German Aircraft of the First World War.* London: Putnam, 1962.
Greer, Louise, and Anthony Harold, *Flying Clothing.* London: Airlife Publications, 1979.
Gunston, Bill, *Fighters, 1914-1945.* Crescent Books, 1978.
Hall, James Norman, and Charles Nordhoff, *The Lafayette Flying Corps,* Vols. 1 and 2. Houghton Mifflin, 1920.
Hawker, Tyrrel Mann, *Hawker, V.C.* London: Mitre Press, 1965.
Hegener, Henri, *Fokker—The Man and the Aircraft.* Aero Publishers, 1961.
Hudson, James J., *Hostile Skies.* Syracuse University Press, 1968.
Immelmann, Franz, *Immelmann, The Eagle of Lille.* London: John Hamilton, 1959.
Imrie, Alex, *Pictorial History of the German Army Air Service, 1914-1918.* London: Ian Allan, 1971.
Jones, H. A., *The War in the Air,* Vols. 2-6. London: Clarendon Press, 1928.
Jones, Ira, *King of the Air Fighters.* London: Ivor Nicholson & Watson, 1934.
Joubert, Philip, *The Fated Sky.* London: Hutchinson, 1952.
Jullian, Marcel, *Nungesser, Le Chevalier du Ciel.* Paris: Le Livre Contemporain.
Lamberton, W. M., *Fighter Aircraft of the 1914-1918 War.* Aero Publishers, 1964.
Lamberton, W. M., *Reconnaissance & Bomber Aircraft of the 1914-1918 War.* Aero Publishers, 1962.

Lewis, Cecil, *Sagittarius Rising.* Collier Books, 1963.
Liddell Hart, B. H., *The Real War, 1914-1918.* Little, Brown, 1930.
Lucas, John, *The Big Umbrella.* London: Elm Tree Books, 1973.
McConnell, James R., *Flying for France.* Doubleday, Page, 1917.
McCudden, James T. B., *Flying Fury.* Folkestone, England: Bailey Brothers and Swinfen, 1973.
Mannock, Edward, *The Personal Diary of Major Edward "Mick" Mannock.* London: Neville Spearman, 1966.
Middlebrook, Martin, *The First Day of the Somme.* W. W. Norton, 1972.
Mitchell, William, *Memoirs of World War I.* Greenwood Press, 1960.
Mortane, Jacques, *Guynemer, the Ace of Aces.* Morrat, Yard & Company, 1918.
Musciano, Walter A., *Eagles of the Black Cross.* Ivan Obolensky, 1965.
Navarre, Jean, *Mes Aventures Guerrieres et Autres.* Paris: L'Édition Française Illustrée, 1920.
Norman, Aaron, *The Great Air War.* Macmillan, 1968.
Nowarra, J. H., *Von Richthofen and the Flying Circus.* Aero Publishers, 1964.
Oughton, Frederick, *Ace with One Eye.* London:

Frederick Muller, 1963.
Parsons, Edwin C., *I Flew with the Lafayette Escadrille.* E. C. Seale, 1937.
Raleigh, Walter, *The War in the Air,* Vol. 1. London: Oxford University Press, 1922.
Read, W. R., *Diary.* London: Imperial War Museum, unpublished.
Reynolds, Quentin, *They Fought for the Sky.* Rinehart, 1957.
Richthofen, Manfred Freiherr von, *The Red Air Fighter.* Arno Press, 1972.
Richthofen, Manfred Freiherr von, *The Red Baron.* Doubleday, 1969.
Rickenbacker, Eddie V., *Fighting the Flying Circus.* Doubleday, 1965.
Robertson, Bruce, ed., *Air Aces of the 1914-1918 War.* Aero Publishers, 1964.
Robinson, Douglas H., *Giants in the Sky.* University of Washington Press, 1973.
Saunders, Hilary St. George, *Per Ardua, The Rise of British Air Power 1911-1939.* Oxford University Press, 1945.
Simkins, Peter, *Air Fighting, 1914-18.* London: Imperial War Museum, 1978.
Smith, Myron J., Jr., *World War I in the Air.* Scarecrow Press, 1977.
Strange, L. A., *Recollections of an Airman.* London: John Hamilton, 1933.
Taylor, A. J. P., *The First World War.* Capri-

corn Books, 1963.
Taylor, J. W. R., *C.F.S. Birthplace of Air Power.* London: Putnam, 1958.
Taylor, J. W. R., *A History of Aerial Warfare.* London: Hamlyn, 1974.
Taylor, J. W. R., *Pictorial History of the R.A.F.* Arco, 1974.
Tuchman, Barbara W., *The Guns of August.* Macmillan, 1962.
Udet, Ernst, *Ace of the Iron Cross.* Doubleday, 1970.
Van Haute, André, *Pictorial History of the French Air Force,* Vol. 1. London: Ian Allan, 1974.
Werner, Johannes, *Knight of Germany.* Arno Press, 1972.
Weyl, A. R., *Fokker, the Creative Years.* Funk & Wagnalls, 1965.
Woodhouse, Jack, *The War in the Air, 1914-1918.* London: Almark Publishing, 1974.

Periodicals
Bruce, J. M., *Air Enthusiast,* No. 9, 1979.
Cross & Cockade Journal, Vols. 2-18, Nos. 1-4, 1961-1977, The Society of World War I Aero Historians, Whittier, California.
Cross & Cockade Journal, Great Britain, Vol. 6, No. 3, 1975, The Society of World War I Aero Historians, Farnborough, Hampshire, England.
Osman, W. H., *Aeronautical Digest,* Vol. 2, 1923.

Picture credits

The sources for the illustrations in this book are listed below. Credits from left to right are separated by semicolons, from top to bottom by dashes. Endpaper (and cover detail, regular edition): Frank Wootton, England.
6, 7: University of California-Riverside, Keystone Mast Collection, by permission of T.M. Visuals Industries, Inc., New York. 8, 9: Publifoto Notizie, Milan. 10, 11: Imperial War Museum, London. 12, 13: Courtesy Steve St. Martin Collection. 14, 15: Australian War Memorial, Canberra. 16: Imperial War Museum, London. 18: *Ali Italiane,* Rizzoli, Milan—Giancarlo Costa, painting by Achille Beltrame, courtesy *Domenica del Corriere,* Milan. 20: Bundesarchiv, Koblenz. 21: Heeresgeschichtliches Museum, Vienna—Musée de l'Air, Paris—British Aerospace, Bristol. 22: Map by Frank J. and Clare M. Ford. 23: *Cross and Cockade Journal,* courtesy Charles Woolley Collection. 25: Eileen Tweedy, courtesy Imperial War Museum, London. 27: David Lees, courtesy Sandro Taragni, Milan. 29: Imperial War Museum, London. 30: Radio Times Hulton Picture Library, London—Aviation and Space Division, National Museum of Science and Technology, Ottawa. 31, 34: Imperial War Museum, London. 35: Photo Bulloz, courtesy Musée des Deux Guerres Mondiales/B.D.I.C., Universités de Paris. 36: Imperial War Museum, London. 39: Giancarlo Costa, painting by Achille Beltrame, courtesy *Domenica del Corriere,* Milan. 40: Ben Benschneider, courtesy James J. Parks Collection, except center, Erich Lessing from Magnum, courtesy Heeresgeschichtliches Museum, Vienna. 41: Dmitri Kessel, courtesy Musée de l'Armée, Paris; Ben Benschneider, courtesy James J. Parks Collection (2)—David Lees, courtesy Museo Baracca, Lugo. 42: Ben Benschneider, courtesy James J. Parks

Collection, except center, Derek Bayes, courtesy Royal Air Force Museum, Hendon. 43: Ara Güler, from *Yanki Dergisi,* courtesy The Turkish Airforce Museum, Izmir—Erich Lessing from Magnum, courtesy Heeresgeschichtliches Museum, Vienna; Ben Benschneider, courtesy James J. Parks Collection; Erich Lessing from Magnum, courtesy Wehrgeschichtliches Museum, Rastatt. 44: Henry Groskinsky, courtesy National Air and Space Museum, Smithsonian Institution. 46: Courtesy Steve St. Martin Collection. 48: Stato Maggiore Aeronautica, Rome—Royal Air Force Museum, Hendon. 49: Courtesy Alex Imrie Collection, England—Imperial War Museum, London. 51: Courtesy Steve St. Martin Collection. 53: Erich Lessing from Magnum, courtesy Heeresgeschichtliches Museum, Vienna—Giancarlo Costa, painting by Guido Zanoni, courtesy Museo del Risorgimento, Milan. 54, 55: Eileen Tweedy, courtesy Imperial War Museum, London—Fil Hunter, courtesy National Air and Space Museum, Smithsonian Institution—Fil Hunter, courtesy National Museum of History and Technology, Smithsonian Institution—Erich Lessing from Magnum, courtesy Wehrgeschichtliches Museum, Rastatt (2). 57: Eileen Tweedy, courtesy Imperial War Museum, London. 58: Imperial War Museum, London. 60: *Ali Italiane,* Rizzoli, Milan, courtesy Museo Aeronautico Caproni di Taliedo, Rome—David Lees, courtesy Sandro Taragni, Milan, except center, *Ali Italiane,* Rizzoli, Milan. 62: Courtesy Steve St. Martin Collection. 64, 65: Drawings by John Batchelor. 67-69: Prints and Photographs Division, Library of Congress. 71: Bundesarchiv, Koblenz; courtesy Steve St. Martin Collection. 72: Musée de l'Air, Paris. 73: Bundesarchiv, Koblenz—Imperial War Museum, London. 74: Courtesy Steve St. Martin Collection—National

Archives, 111-SC-16822. 75: U.S. Air Force Photo Depository—courtesy A. E. Ferko. 76: Painting by Achille Beltrame, courtesy *Domenica del Corriere,* Milan. 79: Imperial War Museum, London. 81: Musée de l'Air, Paris. 82: Imperial War Museum, London; H. Roger-Viollet, Paris; courtesy Steve St. Martin Collection—Musée de l'Air, Paris. 83: Musée de l'Air, Paris; H. Roger-Viollet, Paris—The Bettmann Archive; courtesy Steve St. Martin Collection. 84, 85: Photo Bibliothèque Nationale, Paris. 87: Map by Frank J. and Clare M. Ford. 88, 89: Éditions de l'*Illustration.* Paris. 90: E.C.P. Armées, Ivry-sur-Seine—Imperial War Museum, London. 91-93: Imperial War Museum, London. 94, 95: Drawings by John Batchelor. 97: Henry Groskinsky, courtesy National Air and Space Museum, Smithsonian Institution. 98, 99: Courtesy Sava Mikic and Museum of Yugoslav Aviation, Zemun. 100, 101: Imperial War Museum, London—Ben Benschneider, courtesy L'Escadrille Lafayette Flying Corps Association Collection, United States Air Force Academy Library. 103: National Air and Space Museum, Smithsonian Institution. 104-107: Dmitri Kessel, courtesy Foundation du Mémorial de l'Escadrille Lafayette, Marnes-la-Coquette. 108-111: Imperial War Museum, London. 112, 113: Imperial War Museum, London, inset, A. C. Cooper, courtesy Imperial War Museum, London. 114, 115: Imperial War Museum, London. 116: Bundesarchiv, Koblenz. 118: Arthur L. Newman Collection of Aeronautical Medals, Princeton University Library. 120, 121: Drawing by John Batchelor. 122: Erwin Böhm, courtesy Wolfgram Eisenlohr, Weinheim—Erich Lessing from Magnum, courtesy Wehrgeschichtliches Museum, Rastatt. 124: E.C.P. Armées, Ivry-sur-Seine. 126: Bundesarchiv, Koblenz, except top right, courtesy Steve St. Martin Collection, and bottom right, courtesy A. E. Ferko. 127: Courtesy JG 71 "Richthofen," Wittmund; Bundesarchiv, Koblenz—courtesy A. E. Ferko—Bundesarchiv, Koblenz; courtesy A. E. Ferko; Musée de l'Air, Paris. 129: Fil Hunter, courtesy National Air and Space Museum, Smithsonian Institution (2); Derek Bayes, courtesy Derek G. Arthur Collection, England—Museo Aeronautico Caproni di Taliedo, Rome—Erich Lessing from Magnum, courtesy Wehrgeschichtliches Museum, Rastatt; Ben Benschneider, courtesy James J. Parks Collection; Erich Lessing from Magnum, courtesy Heeresgeschichtliches Museum, Vienna. 130, 131: Drawings rendered by Jim Alexander. 133: Imperial War Museum, London. 134: National Archives, 165-GK-486. 135: Erich Lessing from Magnum, courtesy Heeresgeschichtliches Museum, Vienna—Deutsches Museum,

Munich. 136: Courtesy B. C. Lombard, Hamburg. 137: Bundesarchiv, Koblenz. 139: Courtesy Steve St. Martin Collection. 140-145: Imperial War Museum, London. 146: Fil Hunter, courtesy National Museum of History and Technology, Smithsonian Institution. 148, 149: United States Air Force Museum—David Lees, courtesy Sandro Taragni, Milan. 150, 151: Imperial War Museum, London. 153: National Archives, 111-SC-29656. 154, 155: Drawings by John Batchelor. 156: Imperial War Museum, London—courtesy JG 71 "Richthofen," Wittmund. 157: Courtesy A. E. Ferko. 158: Courtesy Chaz Bowyer Collection, England—Imperial War Museum, London; courtesy Chaz Bowyer Collection, England—Imperial War Museum, London; courtesy Chaz Bowyer Collection, England, and Vice Admiral Sir Lancelot Bell-Davies, KBE; courtesy Chaz Bowyer Collection, England. 159: Courtesy Chaz

Bowyer Collection, England (2); courtesy Mrs. Frank H. McNamara—Imperial War Museum, London (3)—Imperial War Museum, London, except center, Public Archives Canada, Ottawa, C-27808—Imperial War Museum, London (3). 160: Imperial War Museum, London; Musée de l'Air, Paris. 161: Imperial War Museum, London. 162, 163: Drawings by John Batchelor. 164: Steichen Archives, The Museum of Modern Art, New York, by permission of Joanna T. Steichen. 165: Edward Steichen, courtesy Helios Art, Inc., copied by Lee Boltin. 166, 167: United States Air Force Museum. 168, 169: Süddeutscher Verlag, Bilderdienst, Munich. 170: Charles Phillips, courtesy National Air and Space Museum, Smithsonian Institution. 171: U.S. Air Force Photo Depository. 172, 173: Tom Tracy, by permission of Guy Brown Wiser. 175: H. Roger-Viollet, Paris. 176-185: Imperial War Museum, London.

Index

Printed in U.S.A.